In Pursuit of
SAINT
DAVID

In honour of John Wyn Evans,
retired bishop of St Davids
and his successor, Joanna Penberthy

In Pursuit of
SAINT DAVID

PATRON SAINT OF WALES

Gerald Morgan

First impression: 2017
© Gerald Morgan & Y Lolfa Cyf., 2017

Cover design: Y Lolfa
Cover picture: South window of
Church of Saint Padarn, Llanbadarn Fawr

ISBN: 978 1 78461 372 3

Published and printed in Wales
on paper from well-maintained forests by
Y Lolfa Cyf., Talybont, Ceredigion SY24 5HE
e-mail ylolfa@ylolfa.com
website www.ylolfa.com
tel 01970 832 304
fax 832 782

Then David rose, a venerable Seer,
In Sanctity of Life without a Peer...

Nathaniel Griffith, *The Leek* (1717)

The Glorious Ancient British Saint Behold,
David the Great in Fames Records Inroll'd...

Anonymous eighteenth-century ballad

Contents

Acknowledgements

This may be a short book, but I have incurred many debts of gratitude:

To the staff of the National Library of Wales, and the Hugh Owen Library at Aberystwyth University; to Mr Rob Francis and other members of staff at the Information Services Department of Aberystwyth University; and the Numismatics Department of the National Museum of Wales;

To the following church administrators and establishments: the diocesan offices of the cathedrals of St Davids, Hereford, Exeter and Truro; the Very Reverend Jonathan Lean (dean of St Davids); Ruth Wilson, administrator of the Cathedral Church of St David, Hobart, Tasmania; Dr Raymond Refausse of the Church in Ireland; the National University of Ireland; Mr David Galloway of St David's Church, Airmyn, Yorkshire; Ms Andrea Patterson of St David's Church, Kilsallaghan, Ireland;

To friends and fellow-workers in, and beyond, Aberystwyth: Dr Cathryn Charnell-White, Mr Arthur Chater, Dr Mary-Ann Constantine, Ann Corkett, Dr Iestyn Daniel, Mr Robert Davies, the Reverend Canon Jeffrey Gaener, Dr Bruce Griffiths, Dr Heather James, Rhys Kaminski-Jones, Professor Barry Lewis, Mme Yvonne Malléjac of Dirinon, Morfydd Owen, Dr David

Saint David in Dirinon church, Brittany, late medieval. Beside him Saint Anthony of Egypt, whose strict monastic practices David followed.

Parsons, Dr Eryn Mant White. I'm also in debt to Professor Raymond Gillespie of Maynooth and Professor Jonathan Wooding of Sydney University, and to Ken Murphy of the Dyfed Archaeological Trust. Anthony Bentham provided the photograph of John Petts's statue of Saint David in the Catholic church at Briton Ferry, and Alan Hale the photograph of Llanbadarn Fawr church.

I owe special debts of gratitude to Chris and Eleanor Davison who made it possible for me to visit Dirinon and Saint-Divy in Brittany, and for illustrations to this volume. I'm also grateful to my wife Enid who read the original Welsh typescript and made many corrections and suggestions. Dr Karen Jankulak also made many valuable recommendations.

I am much indebted to my editor Eirian Jones and the staff of Y Lolfa Press, who also published the Welsh-language original of this book, to which I have been able to make a few additions and corrections.

Gerald Morgan
February 2017

Introduction

'Who *was* Saint David?' 'What did he ever *do*?' 'Why is his name different in Welsh?' 'The usual Welsh version of David is *Dafydd*, so why is he called *Dewi* in Welsh? What's going on?' Questions like these torment a number of people as 1 March approaches. They have agreed in a moment of weakness to address a St David's Day meeting, and now they have no idea what to say. Some may be bothered by a feeling of hypocrisy: 'How can I raise a glass of wine to toast a man famous for drinking nothing but water?'

It's easy to sympathise. I've experienced St David's Day suppers where the menu was leek *cawl* and apple pie, with tea or lemonade to drink. But the kindness of others has seen me dine at high tables in the Savoy Hotel and the Guildhall in London, feasting with hundreds of the London Welsh on sumptuous dishes and excellent wines. Occasions like these go back three hundred years at least, and they should be cherished.

But the speech-maker or toast-giver must be pitied. After all, Saint David lived a long, long time ago. Historians today don't like to refer to the Dark Ages or the Age of the Saints any more; they prefer to speak of the Early Medieval period. But to us looking back to the sixth century the period is indeed dark: so few are the texts, so difficult much of the archaeology. Children may learn a little about David in Sunday school or primary school, but it's usually reduced to the traditions of his ascetic monasticism and folk tales like the rising of the earth under his feet at the Synod of Brefi. Even these traditions of David's life have to be censored: it's not easy to explain the supposed rape of David's mother to small children.

For adults engaged to speak to adults it's still difficult because there are so few books to help them. There are children's books in Welsh or English, but if you want stronger stuff, there's very little. There's a valuable booklet by Nona Rees, *St David of Dewisland*, but its main theme is the sacred landscape in and around St Davids. Another interesting booklet is *Dewi Sant: Saint David: Patron of Wales*, written from a Roman Catholic viewpoint by J B Midgley. The most dependable works are those by scholars, but they're mostly expensive and can be heavy going for the non-historian. The best by far is *St David of Wales: Cult, Church and Nation*, edited by J Wyn Evans (bishop of St Davids at the time of writing this book) and Professor Jonathan Wooding, but to read it you must either pay (quite a lot) or find an academic library. It's not a source of material for patriotic or pious addresses, but I couldn't have written this book without its help.

So the purpose of this small volume is to help people know about the many-sided figure who was and is the patron saint of Wales – Saint David – through the centuries. It will attempt to determine what we can know about David – man, saint, patron and legend. It's not possible to make a complicated story simple but,

as far as absolutely possible, this book will be readable
– and some of it really enjoyable. Try not to be startled
when some unexpected surprises emerge. Would
you find it impossible to imagine that the original
David *might* have been a man from Ceredigion, not
Pembrokeshire? Or that he became transformed at one
point into a chivalric knight – and a married man at
that? Heaven forfend! – but press on.

As we look more closely we'll see that, in truth,
David was and is a man for all seasons, and not for his
age or festal day alone. We'll be discussing a shadowy
figure who became a major personage in the medieval
British pilgrim movement. This is a saint whose name
was a war cry on the lips of the fierce Cambro-Norman
invaders of Ireland in 1176. To others, David was a figure
of significance at the Reformation, when some claimed
him as a representative of Christianity, uncorrupted
by Roman Catholic teaching, at a time when England
was pagan. To the fantasist-historian Geoffrey of
Monmouth, David was a nephew of King Arthur, the
successor of Dyfrig as archbishop of Caerleon and then
St Davids. He became a favourite of the Welsh poets
until the Reformation, as well as of Henry Tudor.

To the most zealous Reformers, David was a symbol
of everything they loathed – superstition, idolatry and
ignorance. Pilgrimage to St Davids was broken off and
his shrine in the cathedral ransacked and left empty,
just as the pagan Vikings had treated the place five
centuries earlier. But the less rabid were willing to
tolerate him: David was kept in the calendars of the
Anglican Church, although he lost most of his stature for

a time. But Shakespeare gave him a flash of limelight, and with the eventual establishment of Welsh societies in London, Wales and around the world, he became the obvious toast of patriots. By today you will find his name on colleges, schools, clubs, business centres, concert halls, hotels and hospitals.

So David is a fascinating and complex figure, even as the centuries fashion and refashion him. At the root of it all is another extraordinary man, hardly known to the world at large – Rhygyfarch of Llanbadarn Fawr, near Aberystwyth. He lived five centuries after David. It was he who wrote the *Vita Sancti David* [*The Life of Saint David*], one of the Latin masterpieces of medieval Wales. It had a dramatic effect on the history of Wales for a century and more after Rhygyfarch, and it's the starting point for every study of David.

It should be understood that *David* is the subject of this book, not St Davids, the city and its magnificent cathedral, although there must be necessary references to them. For lack of space, there is comparatively little about David's mother, Saint Non. With so much by way of introduction, let's go in pursuit of that protean figure of Welsh history and legend, Saint David – Dewi Sant.

1

Saint David
in his Own Times

The simplest way of viewing David in his own lifetime is not to delve straight into such ancient documents as survive, but to begin with the traditions about him – what people *like* to believe about him. It's true that eventually we shall turn to Rhygyfarch and his *Life of Saint David* in detail, and he will have to be mentioned in this chapter, since some of the traditions derive from his work.

The traditions about David can be summarised as follows:

David was born in Dyfed, son of Sant, king of Ceredigion, and Non, a virtuous nun. Non was raped by Sant and became pregnant. A local lord was told by his cunning men that the baby would become lord of all the land. The lord decided to kill the baby, but was frustrated by a storm. The baby was delivered safely, and was baptised David.

David was educated at *Vetus Rubus*; he went on to establish churches and monasteries in England and Wales. After returning to *Vetus Rubus*, he moved with some of his disciples to *Vallis Rosina* and founded a monastery beside the river Alun, now the site of St Davids cathedral.

There David came into conflict with Baia, a hostile local lord, and his hateful wife, but they were destroyed by God. The discipline in his monastery was strict: work was hard, vegetables and water were the only sustenance allowed. David went to Jerusalem and was ordained archbishop there. He returned, and saved the country from the Pelagian heresy. This he achieved at the Synod of Brefi, where the earth rose under his feet as he preached; on it Llanddewibrefi church now stands, and David was proclaimed archbishop. At another meeting, the Synod of Victory, he was acclaimed bishop. He died at a great age on 1 March, a Tuesday.

This essentially literary tradition is reinforced by features in the local landscape around St Davids: its beauty reinforces an atmosphere of sanctity which delights visitors. It can be summarised as follows:

The site of St Davids cathedral is very different to that of the great English cathedrals, which are surrounded by urban development. Although it has its own mini-city, church and city are mutually invisible, so the cathedral is surrounded by rural peace. The views, either from the high entrance-gate or the church porch, are green. True, the great church, the ruined palace and the Dean's house are visible, but otherwise the scene is of meadow and trees. Ancient walls still surround the consecrated ground, within which fugitives could seek refuge from the law or their enemies.

Beyond the little city is a broader landscape full of sites which, before the Reformation, drew many pilgrims. There is Non's well and ancient chapel; at Porth Clais is David's well where the saint was baptised – it is now a ruin. To the west one passes the remains of St Justinian's chapel on the way down to Porthstinan. From here one can cross the turbulent strait to Ramsey Island (Ynys Dewi), which had other chapels and where the grave memorial of Sadyrnfyw Hael, a bishop who died in 831, was found. Walking northward along the coast path brings one to Porth Mawr (Whitesands Bay), and next to it the site of St Patrick's chapel.

The whole atmosphere of the area is extraordinarily seductive to those open to it, even before one enters the glorious cathedral.

In spite of all this, it is easy to doubt everything and say, as a historian friend once said to me, that what we know of David's life could be written on the back of a postage stamp. After all, Rhygyfarch's *Life*, written so long after the saint's death, is full of incredible miracles and the place names he notes are disputable. So let's begin by putting a handful of possible facts on the table, however hard that may be. Why hard? Because our knowledge is so scanty, because some 'facts' are debatable and because the sources are difficult.

First of all, David *existed*; he was a man of flesh and blood. A few of the early Welsh saints may indeed have been the creations of misunderstandings in the distant past, but nobody doubts that David really lived. Secondly, he is always associated with the early Welsh kingdoms of Dyfed (today's Pembrokeshire) and Ceredigion. It's true that there are medieval churches dedicated to him in Powys, Glamorgan, Gwent, Herefordshire and the counties of south-west England, as well as further afield. Clearly he was born, lived and died in south-west Wales. That is where the earliest

Ramsey Island (Ynys Dewi).

churches dedicated to him can be found; that is the location of his chief sanctuary, St Davids. The usual medieval name for the place in Welsh was *Mynyw*; in Latin, *Menevia*.

A third fact. The Hebrew name David derives from the Old Testament. Therefore those responsible for his baptism must have been Christians. By that time Wales had been Christianised, and so thoroughly that few legends about paganism survived in Welsh tradition. Other Welshmen of his time had been given Biblical names, for example Saint Samson. But there is something special about the Welsh form of his name – Dewi. Now *David* in most parts of Wales became *Dafydd* in Welsh. But *Dewi* comes from the dialect of south-west Wales. This can be shown by looking at modern Welsh words

such as *mynydd* and *gilydd*. In that dialect, the final
–*dd* vanishes, and those words become *mwni* and *gili*.
So David certainly has his origins in south-west Wales,
where that dialect is still in use. Rhygyfarch notes that
the saint was baptised *Davidus*, 'but the common people
called him Dewi'.

Christianity first came to Wales through Roman
influence. It used to be thought that the Roman
occupation of Wales was largely military, and that it
had hardly touched Pembrokeshire. But our knowledge
keeps developing: a Roman fort was recently identified
in Pembrokeshire (at Wiston, near the castle) and
a Roman villa has been excavated in Ceredigion's
Ystwyth valley. The Roman influence in Wales was
more thorough than we used to think. Moreover, when
Rome withdrew her legions, other influences came
from the Mediterranean along the western seaways
to Cornwall, Wales and Ireland, and these would have
been Christian in origin.

Another fact: David lived his life in the sixth century.
This is where facts become complicated! The earliest
mention of David in a Welsh document comes in the
Annales Cambriae, a list of dates with events attached
to them which was kept at St Davids: the oldest copy
was written down in the tenth century. This has an entry
claiming that, in 458, 'David was born in the thirtieth
year after Patrick left Menevia'. Now 458 is, of course,
in the fifth century, not the sixth. Unfortunately for the
facts, the *Annales* was influenced by a legend.

The legend, repeated later by Rhygyfarch, tells that
Saint Patrick came to Menevia intending to evangelise

the people there. Now Patrick certainly lived in the early fifth century, and there was a strong tradition that he had been at Menevia, hence the Patrick chapel at nearby Traeth Mawr (Whitesands Bay). Why then did he go to Ireland – which he certainly did – wherever he may have started from? The legend claimed that an angel told him that Menevia had been set aside by divine purpose for a man who would not be born for another thirty years. So Patrick left for Ireland. The legend is simply a typical medieval attempt to explain the unknown. Whether the chapel was named for the legend or the legend developed from the chapel at Whitesands Bay is open to speculation.

This certainly shipwrecks our expectations, if any, of historical accuracy in Rhygyfarch's work. Because, as we shall see shortly, we know that David died in the late sixth century, and Rhygyfarch knew that too. So he had

to explain that David had died at the age of 147! That figure didn't bother him or his early hearers: after all, according to the Old Testament, the patriarch Joseph had lived to the same age, 147. Miracles certainly happened in the Age of Faith – the Old Testament said so, as well

Early medieval cross-marked gravestone, St Patrick's Chapel.
© Dyfed Archaeological Trust

21

as the New. Unfortunately there is no real evidence for the date of David's birth, so we must turn to enquire for the date of his death. This was of real importance for a saint's *Life*.

First, we note that it is always attributed to 1 March; moreover, Rhygyfarch insists that the 1 March on which David died was a Tuesday. Should we believe any of this? The death of a noted man, with a reputation over a considerable area for his personal sanctity and leadership, would have been a major event among his followers. They would treasure the memory of his dying, the day when they believed he had entered into the joy of the Kingdom of God. So the day of the year would have been memorable, to be kept as a church feast day. As for Tuesday, it's true that in Welsh the third month of the year is *Mawrth*, and Tuesday is *Dydd Mawrth*, both derived from the same Latin name *Mars*, so it might have been Rhygyfarch's perception of the echo as divine coincidence: after all, days and dates vary from year to year. But since that coincidence happens every few years, Rhygyfarch's tradition may be genuine.

For documentary confirmation of David's death we must turn to Ireland where he was a well-known figure, respected in later times for his wisdom: he is described as *doctor sapiens*. There was much coming and going between Wales and Ireland during the medieval centuries, and knowledge of early Irish-Welsh contacts is evident in Rhygyfarch's work. (The important Pembrokeshire saint, Brynach, was an Irishman, although he is never mentioned in connection with David.) The early *Annals of Inisfallen* give the date of David's death as 589, and it is a fact that in that year, 1 March indeed fell on a Tuesday. So, although we cannot be certain, 589 is certainly a reasonable date, which suggests that David may have been born between 520 and 540.

So far, therefore, we have assembled a number of credible statements: about David's home area in south-west Wales, about his baptismal name, the century and the faith into which he was born and his probable lifespan, as well as there being apparent connections with Ireland. So far so good. What about some more facts: who were his parents, where was he born, where did he pass his life, what work did he do? This is where more serious difficulties creep in.

At this point I should signal a spoiler alert: if the traditional version of David's life pleases you, and you do not wish to be disillusioned, please skip to chapter 2!

*

We'll start with David's parents. Rhygyfarch is quite clear about this: they were Sant, king of Ceredigion, and Non, a virtuous nun. Now 'Sant' is an odd name, since it simply means 'saint' in Welsh, borrowed from the Latin *Sanctus*. In the oldest genealogy of the kings of Ceredigion there is nobody named 'Sant', nor anywhere else for that matter. Another most unusual feature is that David is conceived in the body of a virtuous nun. Since we are to assume that she gave no consent, she must have been raped by Sant, as indeed Rhygyfarch tells us. Is 'Sant', therefore, an invention, a title to excuse his behaviour? And does the original storyteller endow him with the kingship of Ceredigion because it pleased the writers of saints' lives that their heroes were of royal blood?

Indeed, many of the Welsh saints have genealogies reaching back to shadowy royal figures of the fifth century, mostly either to Cunedda or Brychan Brycheiniog. These lineages had been drawn up before or during the twelfth century and, while not necessarily reliable, they certainly reflect an important truth: it would have needed men of status and influence to be able to establish churches and draw followers to them.

If Sant is an invented name, what of Non, or Nonnita as Rhygyfarch gives her name? It simply means 'nun', and is also open to dismissal as an invention. This should not concern a historian overmuch: the parentage of royalty and of landholders was important, but the gap of time in Wales between saints and saints' written *Lives* was always long. It was their real or supposed achievements that mattered most to the writers of saints' lives.

It is of course true that Non certainly differs from Sant in having a hinterland. We know nothing else of him at all, but Non exists in place names (Llan-non in Ceredigion, and again in Carmarthenshire). There are churches dedicated to Non in Wales, Cornwall and Brittany, and there is a Breton verse-drama, 'The Life of Saint Non' (see chapter 8). Moreover, Non appears in the genealogies as daughter of Cynyr 'of Caer Gawch in

Mynyw', wheoever he was. But even this back-story is rather thin.

Equally suspicious is the rape story. Although the usual behaviour of a saintly virgin is to prefer death to violation, unless her attacker is struck by paralysis, the story of Non is not unique: Saint Kentigern's mother, according to his *Life*, was also raped and gave birth to the saint, but she was not considered a saint. It all tastes strongly of folk-motif, where the hero's birth takes place in remarkable circumstances involving prophecies, an unusual conception, and a threat of violence to the infant. We may be reminded of the Gospel narratives, where Joseph doubts the paternity of the child-not-yet-born, where Herod menaces the child once he is born, and prophecies surround the tale.

*

What then of the places associated with David? *Mynyw* is a Welsh borrowing from the Irish *muine*, meaning a grove, and there are other place names of Irish origin in south-west Wales. But we may be confused to find that Rhygyfarch never mentions Mynyw/Menevia. He refers instead to *Vallis Rosina* as the site of David's great monastery (and therefore the subsequent cathedral), and *Vetus Rubus*, which means 'the old grove' (perhaps a blackberry patch) as the place where David gained his early education. Gerald of Wales, writing a century after Rhygyfarch, was the first to suggest that *Vetus Rubus* could be identified with the name of Henfynyw – Old Menevia – a church just south-west of Aberaeron, and the identification is widely accepted by scholars.

Since Rhygyfarch tells us that David moved his original monastery from *Vetus Rubus* ('Old Menevia') to *Vallis Rosina*, we might presume that the latter was, so to speak, New Menevia. Of course that name is not historical, but it helps us distinguish the place of David's first monastery as the original Mynyw/Menevia in Ceredigion, which became *Old* (*Vetus*) Menevia which was perhaps near the home of Non's putative father Cynyr of Caer Gawch. But although we shall in due course come across Non's burial place, it is possible that the names of David's real parents had been forgotten and had to be invented for the sake of the story.

This is moving a long way from 'the facts' as I set out to establish them, but it is the very nature of early Welsh history to pose such difficulties. There are more! Consider the implications: David's father is represented as being of Ceredigion, and so possibly was his mother. The saint himself is educated in Ceredigion and establishes his first monastery at *Vetus Rubus*. It's as if Rhygyfarch – himself of Llanbadarn Fawr, Ceredigion – was anxious to emphasise David's connection with that kingdom. Moreover, the most significant event of the *Life*, the Synod of Brefi, is clearly identified as happening at Llanddewibrefi, Ceredigion, the site of an early 'David' church.

Why then is Sant supposed to have met Non in Dyfed, the kingdom south-west of Ceredigion? Obviously Rhygyfarch knew, well before his time, that David's cult was centred in Dyfed. It's worth remembering that Rhygyfarch is vague about the location of David's birth and of his burial. Is it possible that Henfynyw was David's original birthplace and home, as well as the situation of his first monastery? Then may follow the suggestion that, at some time *after his death*, his monastery was moved to a new site, known to Rhygyfarch as *Vallis Rosina*, the valley of the river Alun, although he tells us that the Britons (that is, the Welsh) called it Hodnant.

*

The main problem with this argument is that it defies Occam's razor, the simpler explanation that David himself moved the monastery. Even the mere suggestion that David was a Cardi must surely trouble many Welsh people, believing as they do that – wherever he was educated – he belongs firmly in the present sacred landscape around St Davids. It will surely not be easy to persuade people that both the child David and the mature saint surely belong originally in Ceredigion. Certainly, his cult as a major figure in the Christianity of south-west Wales and beyond has long been identified with St Davids. With its nearby harbours, it is clearly a better site for contact between Wales and Ireland and with Cornwall than is Henfynyw. The area seems always to have been well-populated and richer than Ceredigion, which is traditionally perceived as being poor.

Rhygyfarch of course claims that David himself moved his monastery to what is now the cathedral site, naming it as *Vallis Rosina*. But if we suppose for a moment that David actually lived and died in

St David's church, Henfynyw, Aberaeron.

Ceredigion, when could the transfer have been made? Ceredigion ceased to be an independent kingdom in 871, which could have been the motive for a move. From then on it was part of Seisyllwg (roughly Ceredigion and Carmarthenshire), which itself became part of the new kingdom of Deheubarth in the tenth century, incorporating Dyfed (Pembrokeshire).

Before dismissing the possibility of David's origin in Ceredigion, it is worth looking at the churches of the county. There are churches dedicated to David in Henfynyw itself of course, at Llanddewi Aberarth, Maenordeifi (just south of the Teifi, it's true), Bangor Teifi, Bridell, Henllan, Capel Dewi (Llandysul), Llannarth, Blaenpennal and Llanddewibrefi. Now it's not claimed for a moment that Dewi established these churches – patently he did not: saints don't dedicate churches in their own names. Nevertheless, these churches are witness to the great strength of his cult between the valleys of the Teifi and the Wyre in mid Ceredigion. That strength is much greater in Ceredigion than in the *cantref* or district of Dewisland, where the only 'David' church is the cathedral itself. Moreover, the sacred landscape around St Davids is remarkably devoid of early, that is, from the fifth to the seventh century, Christian monuments. None of this *proves* that David's origins were in Ceredigion, but the point is worth consideration.

It's true that Henfynyw has little to offer by way of evidence of antiquity. But although the church is a Victorian rebuild, the site is clearly ancient. The churchyard is capacious, and there is an early Christian monument, a stone bearing the male name Tigeirn, dating from the period 600 to 800. That alone is enough to suggest the antiquity of the site, though any traces of an early church must survive only under the present building.

The suggestion that David may have been a Ceredigion man is not new. The possibility is advocated by the retired bishop of St Davids, the Very Reverend J Wyn Evans, a leading scholar in the study of early religion in Wales. He suggested to me that I should discuss the possibility, while acknowledging that certainty is not possible. Nor is he the first to have suggested it. In a St David's Day address in 1910, reported in the *Cambrian News*, the antiquarian George Eyre Evans challenged his listeners thus:

If, he said, he threw down the gauntlet that their national saint was a Cardiganshire man, he would not be far wrong.

It was probably he who was responsible for three anonymous articles on folklore in the *Welsh Gazette* in 1912 which argued that David was a Cardi.

We may now move back from speculation to fact. Whether David himself re-established his monastery on the cathedral site as Rhygyfarch claimed, or whether it was moved later, Rhygyfarch is keen to emphasise the nature of David's monastic discipline, which is described as extremely ascetic and self-sacrificial. We are given a long and detailed account of daily life there: monks ploughing (without animals) using breast-ploughs, the utter rejection of personal possessions, the diet of vegetables and water, chastity, and the complete subjection of individuality. Only guests and the sick are given indulgence. It was thus that David gained, long before Rhygyfarch's day, the epithet *Aquaticus*, the water drinker. Many scholars today are inclined to accept this as a genuine description. Gildas, writing in the sixth century, fiercely attacked that kind of monastic discipline, arguing that it was unreasonably harsh. Although he doesn't name David, his very phrases are echoed in the description of that discipline given by Rhygyfarch centuries later.

*

Monastic discipline is the main achievement that we can attribute to the historical David. So much else is legendary, a matter of prophecy and miracle. Therefore are there any other facts about his life that we can trust? David's great achievement, according to Rhygyfarch, is of course the Synod of Brefi, called to defeat the Pelagian heresy. In order that he could be heard, the ground rises under David, making his address audible to the multitude. By Rhygyfarch's time, and for several centuries before, Llanddewibrefi had been a major David church. It stands on a low hill, which indeed gives a somewhat artificial impression which would call for an explanation. The miracle is of course the 'explanation' of the hill.

The Pelagian heresy had been defeated in Britain in the fifth century by Saint Germanus (Garmon) of Auxerre, especially called from Gaul to aid the British Church. That triumph was itself explained by the miracle of the Alleluia Victory. To demonstrate David's spiritual power, Rhygyfarch used the 'miraculous' hillock of Brefi to explain how David could have achieved a similar triumph to that of Germanus a century earlier. There is in fact no evidence of a revival of Pelagianism in the sixth century, but David's reputation could be boosted by the miracle of the hill and the many other miracles noted by Rhygyfarch. In particular, David's success at the Synod affirms his proclamation as archbishop of Britain. As is clear from his text, the claim to the archbishopric is the underlying agenda of Rhygyfarch's work. There is in fact no other evidence for David having been either a bishop or archbishop: what we know of the early Welsh Church portrays its major figures as abbots, not bishops, except with hindsight.

*

It is inevitable that modern scholarship and attitudes make inroads into the traditional figure of David. We do not credit the figures of Sant and Non as his parents; we do not believe in miracles of the kind that were common belief in earlier centuries. Professor Barry Lewis has demonstrated that David's so-called sister, Magna, was a fiction. Geoffrey of Monmouth invented a family relationship for David with King Arthur. But we are left with the figure, however shadowy, of a real man living in south-west Wales in the sixth century: he was a Christian leader and ascetic who inspired generations to cherish his name and follow his ideals.

What of the times in which David lived? It was a remarkable age, full of extreme changes. Although Rome had lost its grip on Britain a century before David's time, it had left its powerful impact on the landscape (roads, forts, towns, villas) and on the people – their language, their culture, and their Christianity. Britain in the sixth century saw much movement and migration. Settlers from Europe – the Angles and Saxons – had landed on Britain's eastern and southern shores, looking for room to settle and farm, and they spoke Germanic dialects.

Others were anxious to move *from* Britain and settle on the Continent, such as those taking their British language with them to Brittany. From Ireland came migrants to west Wales and north-west Scotland. They continued to speak their own Irish in Wales for several generations, leaving their names carved in their Ogam alphabet. Dyfed was actually ruled for a time by Irishmen of the Deisi people.

Through all this we should remember that there

was at this time no such entity as *Cymru* or Wales. The words can only be used in respect of the peninsula which now contains Wales as a geographical term. In David's time the peninsula was part of a chain of realms which stretched from the rivers Clyde and the Forth all the way down to Cornwall and eventually Brittany, with the people speaking mutually comprehensible British dialects. These would eventually develop into new and separate languages – Breton, Cornish, Welsh and Cumbrian. If we accept that the Saxons began settling in the east of the island about AD 400, it took their settlements over a century and a half to reach far enough west to cut Wales off from the Britons of the south-west and the north-west, though contacts between them were not lost.

What then of south-west Wales, Ceredigion and Pembroke, before and during the age of David? By the saint's birth, around 520–40, Christianity had spread through the Welsh peninsula. The expression 'the Age of the Saints' is no long current among historians, but there is little doubt that preaching, witnessing and establishing churches and monasteries did actually happen, and that paganism faded away. No doubt collective memory simplified and distorted what actually happened: inventing some 'saints' who were never people of flesh and blood, and attributing supernatural powers to some who were. But most of them were real men and women whose names lived on in tradition and public reverence, so that they were eventually commemorated as saints in popular imagination.

But where were the churches of these early Christians in Wales? Where are the ruins of the first monasteries? In Ireland the Gallarus Oratory and the churches of Glendalough survive from the pre-conquest era: in England many Saxon churches survive in whole or part, like St Peters-on-the-Wall in Essex, Escomb Church in County Durham, the monastery of Saint Paul, Jarrow, in Tyne and Wear, and the ancient church at Bradford on Avon, Wiltshire. Why is there nothing similar in Wales? Put simply, the Welsh did not build churches from stone but from timber. Pre-Norman stonework exists only in Presteigne, Powys: it was under Norman influence that the oldest surviving stone churches in Wales were built – in the south at Chepstow, Llantwit Major and Ewenny, or by the princes of Gwynedd at Penmon, Aberffraw, Llanaber and Tywyn (Meirionethshire).

For earlier visible remains the historian in Wales must turn to the carved stone monuments of the pre-Norman age. The earliest (fifth to the sixth century) are those which bear only the name of an individual (sometimes with his father's name) – probably gravestones. The names are in Latin or Irish form, the latter often in the Ogam alphabet either alone or with a Latin version. After 700 the majority of these stones are either shaped in cross form or with crosses carved on them; inscriptions are rare. The great majority are in Pembrokeshire, probably reflecting the greater availability of carveable stone, and perhaps greater wealth.

What is remarkable about St Davids itself is the lack of these early monuments. The oldest is the cross in

St Non's chapel, dating from between 600 and 800. There are numerous other stones in the cathedral and its vicinity, but all date from 900 to 1100. Does this support the idea that St Davids only became an important Christian centre comparatively late? This could validate the suggestion made above that David's original base was in Ceredigion, not Pembrokeshire. But it's hard to prove a positive from negative evidence.

Whatever the truth of that theory, the next chapter will show how the name and status of David grew in importance between his lifetime and that of Rhygyfarch. Although the traditions about the saint depend greatly on Rhygyfarch's *Life*, that book did not create him. The process was already well under way. In later centuries again, the figure of David would change and grow in ways never contemplated either by David himself or his first biographer.

2

Saint David's Life after Death

In searching for the few reliable facts about David's life, it was obvious that his name had become well-enough known to be mentioned in the early chronicles and saints' lives of Ireland. He was also familiar to people in Brittany. His name appears in the Latin *Life of St. Paul Aurelian,* written in Brittany in the ninth century. There, for the first time, David is described as 'the water drinker'. His development as a Breton saint is described in chapter 8.

Another early piece of evidence is the inscription which partly survives on the wall of Llanddewibrefi church. Today the broken state of the monument and its Latin inscription would be incomprehensible but for the fact that the great Welsh scholar Edward Lhuyd visited the church in 1699, before the stone had been shattered, and recorded what it said:

Here lies Idnerth son of Jacob, killed because of the plundering of Saint David.

Scholars date the memorial to the ninth century,

perhaps earlier. We should understand that what has been plundered is the shrine of David at the church. It is notable for being, almost certainly, the oldest original record mentioning David, and referring to his status as a saint. Presumably Idnerth was killed defending the church, but against whom – Viking, English or Welsh attackers – we cannot know.

Other early facts connect David's name with the English kingdom of Wessex, ruled between 871 and 899 by King Alfred. The king was eager to improve the cultural level of his people: he himself learned Latin, and prepared books in Old English. He sent to St Davids for help, as it was a well-known centre of learning, inviting the Welsh priest Asser to his court. Asser wrote a *Life of Alfred*, referring in it to himself as a man from the far south-west of Wales, and to his relative Nobis, who he says was *archiepicopus* (archbishop) in the monastery and land of St Davids.

Additionally, the monks at Glastonbury claimed that they had 'relics' of Saint David, presumably referring to body parts. Other early English documents refer to David as a saint and bishop, presumably through the influence of Asser, whom Alfred promoted to be bishop of Sherborne.

The Idnerth Stone, Llanddewibrefi.

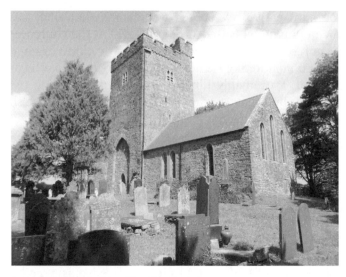

St David's church, Llanddewibrefi.

Towards the end of the first millenium AD David was already being recognised as foremost of the Welsh saints and as an inspiration to the Welsh people. This is clear from the tenth-century Welsh prophetic poem *Armes Prydein Fawr*, the Great Prophecy of Britain (note the word order). It was written to urge the people of Wales, the Cymry (an early use of the word), to join with the men of Cornwall, Ireland and Scotland to rise against the oppression of the Great Tyrant. This refers to Æthelstan, king of England until 939, who was eager to extend his lordship over the whole archipelago of Britain and Ireland.

The poet claims:

The Welsh will dedicate themselves to God and David…
The enemy will be driven in flight by the prayers of David
    and the saints of Britain…
The Welsh will lead under David's holy banner…
The Irish will demand of the English why they have
    destroyed the rights of David…
David will be leader of the hosts…
He does not die, he does not flee, he does not weary,
He never ends, he does not fail or bend or weaken.

It is an extraordinary tribute to David but, as an appeal, it failed. Hywel Dda (the Good), ruler of most of Wales until his death c.950, followed a policy of cooperation with England. But the poem shows that David was the natural choice as national representative and inspirer of the proposed campaign. This belief in David as a national, even military, leader was to be repeated in later centuries. The poem also demonstrates knowledge of English assaults on David's territory; we know from other sources that the English raided south-west Wales in 777, 783 and 818.

It is impossible to know when David was first recognised as the patron saint of Wales, but it is clear that at least a faction in Wales were doing so in the tenth century, and that no other saint was ever considered for the title. The position in England was very different: at first it was possible for Saint Cuthbert (c.634–687) and the saintly kings Edmund (841–869) and Edward the Confessor (1003–1066) each to play the patron's role in England. Only with the establishment of the Order of the Garter, c.1348, was George, already patron of

39

Portugal, Georgia and Malta, recognised as the patron saint of the English too.

Lastly, the importance of Menevia as David's monastery, at least from the ninth century if not before, is evident from the number of times it was sacked, especially by the Irish Vikings. It's true that other Welsh churches and Christian communities were also attacked, but they cannot compare in suffering with St Davids. We should, however, remember that the principal surviving records were kept at St Davids – Menevia in the chronicles.

810	Menevia burnt
907	Menevia destroyed
982	Menevia sacked
988	Menevia, St Dogmaels, Llanbadarn, Llantwit and Llancarfan sacked
992	Menevia sacked
999	Menevia sacked and Bishop Morgenau killed
1012	Menevia sacked
1022	Menevia destroyed
1073	Menevia sacked and Bishop Bleiddud killed
1080	Menevia sacked and Bishop Abraham killed
1089	David's shrine destroyed
1091	Menevia destroyed

Brut y Tywysogion [*The Chronicle of the Princes*] describes the attack of 1089 thus:

Then was the shrine of David taken from the church and thoroughly despoiled close to the city.

The word *shrine* can mean either the metal container for the saint's relics or the stone structure in which it was kept – clearly the former in this case. We know nothing more of the early shrine of David, but examples of portable Irish shrines survive, made of ornamented metal. Perhaps the monks had been able to hide the container during raids prior to 1089, or it (and the relics) may have been destroyed more than once. It must be assumed that there was little remaining at St Davids at the time of the last Viking raid. But whatever may have happened to David's bones since his death, we shall hear more of his relics in due course: relics and bones are, of course, not necessarily the same thing.

The eleventh century, when St Davids was raided at least six times, was a time of trouble across Wales. The English had already occupied parts of north-east Wales as far as the river Clwyd, and established a borough at Rhuddlan. Then, in 1067, the Normans crossed the river Wye and penetrated well into Gwent and then Glamorgan. The Welsh princes of Gwynedd, Powys, Glamorgan, Gwent and Deheubarth were mostly fighting each other and (some of them) against the invaders too. With the Vikings also active in the west, Wales faced threats and actual conquest.

*

To summarise thus far. There is sufficient evidence to show David's considerable status well before the arrival of the Normans in 1067: the Llanddewibrefi inscription, the evidence of the Irish chronicles, the poem *Armes Prydein Fawr* and the frequent attacks on Menevia. But what of churches? Were there, in Wales, churches dedicated in David's name, apart presumably from Menevia and Llanddewibrefi?

We know little of the churches of Wales before the Norman arrival, but certainly before 1200, men with a devotion to David had consecrated churches in his name. By this time Gwynfardd Brycheiniog had composed his great ode to Saint David (about 1170–80) in which he names nineteen David churches. Despite devotion to other Welsh saints, to the Virgin Mary, and saints Peter and Michael, the number of David churches was still increasing. Dr Heather James lists some fifty-four, besides the cathedral, not including churches in the lordships of south-east Wales (see Appendix I).

And with that, it is time to move on to Rhygyfarch and his book.

3

Rhygyfarch and his Work

Rhygyfarch is known to us as a monk, scholar, poet and author who lived between *c*.1056 and 1099. He was the remarkable son of an exceptional father, Sulien the Wise, head of the religious community at Llanbadarn Fawr in north Ceredigion. The community, often called by historians a *clas*, was a kind of hereditary ecclesiastical corporation, co-owning land which provided for their upkeep. Sulien obeyed the call to become bishop of St Davids, not once but twice. The first time was in 1073 following the murder of Bishop Bleiddud, and he retired in 1078. Following the murder of Bishop Abraham in 1080, he was recalled to the bishopric, retiring again in 1085 and dying in 1091 aged 80. His courage in taking up the appointment twice after the murders of his immediate predecessors is remarkable, as was his scholarship.

Educated in Scottish and Irish monastic schools as well as in Wales, Sulien himself taught his four gifted sons, Rhygyfarch, Ieuan, Arthen and Daniel. The fact that a priest and bishop had four sons may surprise the reader, used to the Roman Catholic ban on priestly marriage, but that only became the Church's teaching from the twelfth century, and even then Welsh priests in the later medieval centuries were not easily persuaded to live alone.

Sulien and his sons stood on the watershed between two difficult periods in the history of Welsh Christianity. Before the Normans they had to endure attacks from both Vikings and English, costing lives and treasure. Llanbadarn Fawr was the last glowing lamp of early Welsh Christian culture, finally extinguished by the Norman invaders in the early twelfth century. These were not raiders but occupiers and colonisers, who brought with them an agenda of Church reform and obedience to Canterbury.

The Welsh Church prior to 1067 had adhered to a decentralised model of organisation, insofar as we understand it. There were bishoprics in St Davids, Bangor and Glamorgan, with no overall authority,

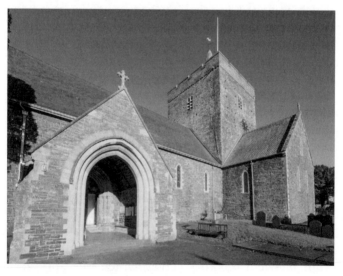

Llanbadarn Fawr church.

Photograph: Alan Hale

that is, no archbishop, and a network of monastic communities and mother churches. New bishops were consecrated by existing bishops. Pre-Norman England had its archbishops at Canterbury and York, but there too the structure of minsters and subordinate chapels was originally not entirely unlike that in Wales. But the Normans would have none of it.

Their reform agenda would recognise Canterbury, but the country was to be thoroughly administered through parishes, archdeaconries and dioceses. English bishops were all replaced sooner or later. The policy was the same for Wales, although it would take much longer to put into full effect. The *clasau* would all be reformed: some became houses of Augustinian canons, like Bardsey and Penmon; Llanbadarn Fawr became briefly a Benedictine priory before a restoration of the *clas*, and then a parish church. New Norman boroughs often had a Benedictine house established, as in Chepstow, Cardiff, Newport and Monmouth. New orders of monks reached Wales, most obviously the Cistercians, while the orders of friars established houses in many towns. As for bishops, the Normans created a fourth diocese, St Asaph, and although sometimes willing to tolerate Welshmen as bishops, they would have to accept full obedience to Canterbury.

As soon as the Normans crossed the river Wye in 1067 they began this process. Sulien would have been well aware of it, although St Davids would not be affected for a while yet. But less than twelve months after his consecration as bishop in 1080, Sulien would have to deal with two problems. First, the turbulent dynastic politics of Gwynedd and Deheubarth reached crisis point. Rhys ap Tewdwr, the exiled claimant to the rule of Deheubarth, returned from Ireland and claimed sanctuary from his rivals at St Davids. Then Gruffudd ap Cynan, exiled from Gwynedd, came to seek Rhys ap Tewdwr's cooperation against their mutual enemies. In Sulien's presence they swore alliance on the relics of Saint David, and were duly victorious. Those may have been the very relics pillaged by the Vikings eight years later. Rhys acknowledged Sulien's diplomatic skills, which were clearly formidable, by granting to St Davids the whole *cantref* of Pebidiog, today called Dewisland, reaching almost as far as Fishguard, and surely the largest single grant ever made by a Welsh prince to the Church.

Then William the Bastard, conqueror of England, arrived, ostensibly on pilgrimage to the famous shrine. Since he landed at the nearest harbour, Porth Clais, he clearly came by sea, a voyage not without risk. According to the *Anglo-Saxon Chronicle*, he brought soldiers with him, and freed many prisoners, whoever they may have been. We know that Sulien, forewarned, went with his clergy to welcome William. It seems evident that the king's real purpose was political. He was not interested in incorporating Wales directly into England; he had stationed his lords on the Welsh March and allowed them considerable rein. But he seems to have acknowledged Rhys ap Tewdwr as ruler of Deheubarth, subject to the annual payment of forty pounds noted in the Domesday Book. William would not for a moment have listened to any special pleading on behalf of St Davids's claim to be an archbishopric, even had anyone dared to suggest it. But it kept its status and privileges, such as they were, for another generation, though a mint for English coinage was established at St Davids (DEVITUN).

So with Sulien well understanding the threat to the ecclesiastical order in Wales, and the destruction already wrought in St Davids itself, he may have already conceived, either at this time or later, a plan to raise the status of St Davids and its patron saint. In 1081 his eldest son, Rhygyfarch, was about twenty-five, and either then or at some time in the coming years he probably asked the young man to write Saint David's *Life*. Rhygyfarch certainly spent time at St Davids; he tells us that he consulted the ancient worm-eaten books in the cathedral's library. Some scholars believe the *Life* may actually have been written after Sulien's death in 1091.

That event is given rich attention in the *Chronicle of the Princes* for that year, an entry whose Latin original could have been written by Rhygyfarch himself, or one of his brothers.

Then died Sulien, bishop of Menevia, the wisest of the Britons and distinguished for his religious life, after the most praiseworthy education of his pupils and the wisest teaching of his churches, in the 80th year of his age, on New Year's Eve.

*

Rhygyfarch's *Vita Sancti David* is a truly remarkable book. There is a summary of the contents in the

Appendix, stripped of the text's high and colourful rhetoric. When I first read it, I was, like so many others, looking for 'the facts, the truth' about David and his life. Surely there must be – in spite of all the miracles – some way of recognising the 'real' Saint David. But reading and rereading it, one comes to realise, that this is not a biography in the Boswellian sense of the word, nor is it modelled on a classical biographer like Plutarch. A realistic biography doesn't begin with prophecies, miracles and names like 'Sant' and 'Non' which sound as though they come from a fifteenth-century miracle play.

What then is this book of Rhygyfarch's? It would be folly to treat it as if it were a fairy story for children, though a careful reading makes it obvious that Rhygyfarch understood how little he actually knew about David. But he had several objectives to achieve. He understood David to have been a man of unblemished life and spiritual power. He had to convey this in a way in which the book can be read, portion by portion, in monasteries. This happened especially on the saint's particular day in the Church calendar as, we shall see, was the custom for centuries. But he had also to convince an audience beyond Wales of the status of this special Welsh man of God who had been an archbishop, and of his monastery at St Davids.

Rhygyfarch had two models in mind. The first was the existing pattern already established in the *Life of St. Martin*; of which more later. But the underlying model is the Gospel pattern. First, of course, one notices inconsistencies within the *Life* just as there are in the four Gospels. Rhygyfarch claims that David founded twelve monasteries, but only nine are named. He is proclaimed archbishop twice, once in Jerusalem and again at the Synod of Brefi. This might be explained by noting the second occasion as a British recognition of the first, but later David is acknowledged as bishop. But to Rhygyfarch's readers, such points would be hairsplitting.

More important is the positive Gospel influence. The hero (Jesus > David) is the subject of prophecies. Both have forerunners (John the Baptist > Patrick). Both have royal ancestors (King David > Cunedda). Both are conceived in special circumstances (Joseph first thinks of Jesus, conceived by the Holy Spirit, as illegitimate > David is the child of rape). A cruel tyrant (Herod > the nameless chieftain, not to be confused with Baia and his wife) plans to kill the baby, but is frustrated.

Thereafter the resemblances are less obvious. Jesus is baptised as an adult, David as a baby; Rhygyfarch believed that infant baptism had become the norm. We know nothing of the education of Jesus, though obviously he had learnt to read, write and debate, and was steeped in knowledge of the Hebrew scriptures. The places where David was educated are named: the first was *Vetus Rubus*, where we are told that David learnt the Psalms, the Biblical readings for the whole year, mass and other services. The second is the island of *Wincdilantquendi*, a name of which we can make no sense. At this place his teacher is named as Paulinus (Welsh *Peulin*). The name is certainly historical: he is supposed also to have taught Saint Teilo, a major figure among the saints of Carmarthenshire, and an early stone at Caeo names the grave of Paulinus. Paulinus figures again in the *Life* as the man who urged the invitation of David to the Synod of Brefi. Rhygyfarch would have been more than ready to credit Paulinus as David's teacher for a special reason. Paulinus was believed to have been a pupil of Saint Germanus of Auxerre, but that is impossible, since Germanus died before 450. But Germanus was famous for his campaign against the Pelagian heresy, rampant on this island in the fifth century. What better teacher than Paulinus for David, whom Rhygyfarch believed had been summoned to the Synod of Brefi to preach against a revived Pelagianism?

There are, of course, major differences between David and Jesus: the saint is credited with a long life, while Jesus was crucified as a young man, a fate which, after the Romans left, is not inflicted on any of the early Welsh saints. David, of course, could perform miracles just as Jesus could – they were a proof of his sanctity: no miracle, no saint! David's miracles are borrowed from both the Old and New Testaments: he can strike the earth and bring forth water; he can live to a great age, like the patriarchs and Moses. He can heal the blind and even bring back the dead boy Magna to life on his way to the Synod of Brefi.

Even in the world of miracles, some seem more whimsical than others. David can swallow poison without dying; he can command Máedóc's bell to return to its owner in Ireland, and immediately an angel obeys. David's enemies are destroyed by fire from heaven. More fancifully, David's pupil Aidan calls back his oxen which fell over a cliff by accident. Stranger still, the Irish Saint Bairre can ride a horse across the sea and meet Saint Brendan on the back of a whale! One has to ask whether Rhygyfarch, who was obviously a sane and clever man, could believe such tall tales. But Rhygyfarch belonged to a different age, when belief in miracles was normal, part of the world of Christian culture; nor was such belief confined to one religion.

Rhygyfarch certainly took pleasure in weaving miracles into his narrative, even embellishing them with details. For example, David's pupil Modomnóc cared for the monastery's beehives. When he sailed to Ireland, the bees followed him, and when filled with longing for his master David's presence, he returned and the bees followed him again. This happened three times, so the saint blesses the bees and commands them to go back to Ireland, so that no bees would ever return to the monastery. Rhygyfarch assures us that he has proved the truth of this with other incredible details. But if Rhygyfarch had visited St Davids – and we can be sure that he had – he would have certainly seen bees! Why, therefore, does he assure us to the contrary? But to ask the question is to miss the point.

So the ostensible purpose of Rhygyfarch's work, therefore, is to fulfil the need for readings for services and mass on 1 March. But, clearly, he intends to glorify David as the greatest of the saints of Wales, and to elevate the status and history of St Davids and its diocese. By demonstrating that David had been an archbishop, it is clearly implied that the see should again have metropolitan status, with power above the other dioceses of Wales. The privileges of David are to be maintained, so that St Davids can offer sanctuary to those who seek it, whether criminals or refugees, such as Rhys ap Tewdwr. No doubt Rhygyfarch, not to mention his father Sulien, had this positive view of the status of St Davids. There was, of course, a tradition that although an early pope had granted a *pallium* (the cloak entitling a bishop to archiepiscopal status) to St Davids, it had been taken to Brittany by Saint Samson. By setting out the claims of David and his see so strongly, Rhygyfarch was consciously laying down fuel for a debate which would burn for a hundred years after his death.

What were Rhygyfarch's sources for his work? Doubtless his father's beliefs would have inspired him, and he would have learnt from him about Ireland and its saints. He tells us that he had held the ancient documents of St Davids in his hands. Certainly one would have been the *Annales Cambriae*, where he would have found the story about the birth of David thirty years after Patrick's departure for Ireland. He would have known of oral traditions about some of the holy places around St Davids, especially perhaps Patrick's chapel at Whitesands Bay. He would also have known about the mound at Llanddewibrefi, supposed to have risen under David's feet at the Synod.

A fundamental question is that of Rhygyfarch's understanding of the nature of sainthood. The answer today to 'what is a saint?' is of course twofold. One may refer to anyone of good deeds and character as a 'saint' without bestowing any mystery on them. But the word has long had a special character in Christian belief. Saints of the Roman Catholic Church are supposedly those who have been determined to be saints by a long process. A saint must be dead; two miracles must have been performed by his or her agency, and the bureaucratic discussion involves an inquiry into any possible blemishes of character or behaviour. Beatification is the first step, followed by canonisation. Thenceforward it is believed that a saint can be prayed to in order that he or she may intercede in heaven. A saint may become patron of all kinds of institutions, from a hospital or a guild to a whole country. A saint can be the object of prayer in the case of all kinds of misfortune, illness or danger.

However, in the early centuries of Christendom there was no bureaucracy in Rome to vet anyone for canonisation. The tradition simply emerged that virtuous men and women of the New Testament were acknowledged as saints. Then followed the men and women martyred in the early years, then the learned teachers and theologians, the Church Fathers. Indeed, if a man or woman were not famous at all, but simply lived an exceptionally virtuous and charitable life, they could be considered – after their deaths – as saints. It then became natural that some might be remembered better than others, and have miracles attributed to them, while others remained in obscurity. Their names might be linked to water sources which became holy wells, probably centres of pre-Christian practices; chapels, crosses and shrines could be raised in their honour.

In Wales between AD 400 and AD 800 many men and a smaller number of women came to be accepted as saints in their own local areas. Many of them are associated with one place only and we know nothing else about them. Others became known over a wider area: Teilo, Beuno, Cadog, Dyfrig, Illtyd, Padarn, Tysilio, and, of course, David.

None of the Welsh saints of the medieval period was ever formally canonised by Rome: they were already saints before the process was formalised. Even David was not, as is sometimes said, canonised by Pope Callistus in 1123: he simply granted special status to St Davids as a place of pilgrimage – twice to Menevia equalled one to Rome. Needless to say, the lack of formal canonisation never impeded the cult of Saint David one jot, either in the medieval Church or in popular esteem.

What then of the writing of saints' *Lives*, the Latin *Vitae*? As we close in on Rhygyfarch's text, we must understand that he is, as noted, following a pattern or model in writing David's *Life*. The first volume of the kind is the *Life of St. Martin*. He was a fourth-century Roman whose *Life* was written by his near-contemporary Sulpicius Severus, another Roman. His intention was to record the virtues and feats of his hero, the purity of his life and the obstacles and temptations he overcame. The nineteenth-century Welsh-language *cofiant* or memoir, usually written about hero-figures of Welsh Nonconformity, performed a similar moral function. The subject's death was usually a special focus of these once-popular volumes.

Sulpicius's pioneering volume about Martin was a pattern for hundreds of saints' *Lives* in Latin and other languages that were written over the following centuries. The writers were keen to establish their particular saint's virtues, and can be numbingly boring, particularly in their repetitions of miracles. But they were necessary: if Jesus and his followers could perform miracles, which nobody doubted, then more recent heroes could obviously do the same.

The minority of the Welsh who were literate certainly knew of saints and their lives before the time of Rhygyfarch. The ninth-century *Historia Brittonum* contains an abbreviated account of Saint Germanus, the conqueror of the Pelagian heresy, and his story was obviously known to Rhygyfarch. Saint Samson's *Life* had been written by a Breton monk in the seventh century, and that of Saint Paul Aurelian in the ninth, again by a Breton. Although documents may have been lost, the first saints' *Lives* we have written by Welshmen come at the end of the eleventh century – David's by Rhygyfarch and that of Saint Cadoc of Llancarfan by Lifris. It seems clear that Rhygyfarch's work was the earlier, and that Lifris had read it, and sought to show that Cadoc was a greater figure than David. For example, Lifris claims that when David was asked by an angel to assemble a synod, he replies that Cadoc is much worthier in every way to carry this out. But the angel replies that Cadoc is otherwise engaged, so David carries out the task. There is no mention of Pelagianism. Lifris's work is three times the length of Rhygyfarch's, and is full of interesting material, but it is not so orderly in its composition.

There is one vital question which must concern anyone who wants to discuss Rhygyfarch's work – which text? Because there are two versions in different manuscripts, both said to be by Rhygyfarch, but one is much shorter than the other. Scholars before the 1960s studied the longer version, but a leading Welsh church scholar of the time, J W James, argued that the shorter version was the original, to which another writer had added material. Scholars more recently have judged that the shorter version is in fact a précis of the longer original. An edited version of the shorter text has been included in *St David of Wales: Cult, Church and Nation*. To further complicate matters, Gerald of Wales produced a version of his own in the twelfth century, with little original material, but showing a real interest in place names.

Nor should we forget the Welsh-language version, *Buched Dewi*, from the *Book of the Anchorite of Llanddewibrefi*, copied in 1346. This remarkable volume also contains a Welsh *Life* of Saint Beuno, principal saint of Gwynedd. *Buched Dewi* is not a translation from the Latin original but a much shorter version for more popular consumption. There are a number of later copies of the Welsh *Life*, showing how popular it was.

Rhygyfarch wrote in Latin, so that church authorities everywhere would be able to read it. If Sulien and other leaders of the Welsh Church were to withstand Norman pressure, they would need to show that there was a valuable Christian heritage in Wales, deserving of respect. Other major works written in Wales in the coming century would be in Latin, such as Geoffrey of

Monmouth's fantasy *Historia Regum Britanniae* [*The History of the Kings of Britain*] and *Leges Wallicae* – the Welsh laws.

The description of David's journey through Wales and England founding monasteries was a convenient way for Rhygyfarch to draw together existing traditions about the places he names. Some of them, at least (for example, Glastonbury, Glascwm and Llangyfelach) had such connections with David. After his travels 'he returned to the place he had left when he began his journey, namely *Vetus Rubus*. His nephew, bishop Gwystli, lived there.' Despite this naming of a nephew, Rhygyfarch pays virtually no attention to David's larger family.

After establishing himself and his monastery in *Vallis Rosina*, Rhygyfarch tells us of David's encounter with the local chieftain, Baia or Boia, and his evil wife. An encounter with a tyrant is a regular element in many saints' *Lives*. In *The Life of St Padarn*, probably written at Llanbadarn, possibly by a brother of Rhygyfarch, the hero Padarn overcomes both Maelgwn and Arthur in the tyrant's role. Rhygyfarch may have taken his tyrant's name from the place name Clegyr Fwya or Caer Fwya, not far from the cathedral. Of course it is also possible that the place was named by someone familiar with Rhygyfarch's work. The episode is ostensibly moral fiction designed to entertain a male audience and includes the sexual antics of the maidservants. This, of course, was entirely in accord with a male clergy culture conditioned to believe in the weakness of the female sex.

Then Rhygyfarch turns to one of the most important parts of his work, the description of the extreme asceticism of the monastic discipline at *Vallis Rosina*. Its foundations, described in detail, are hard work on the land without the use of animals for ploughing, absolute poverty in personal life, regular worship, obedience and self-sacrifice. Many scholars now agree that this is not Rhygyfarch's idealistic imagination at work, but a genuine description of how life was at the early monastery.

This tough way of life is remarkably similar to that described in a tenth-century Latin document from Brittany, 'Excerpts from the Book of Saint David', which also describes a bleakly ascetic monastic discipline. Rhygyfarch himself refers to David's monks living 'like the monks of Egypt', and early monasticism in Egypt was indeed quite ferociously hard. Rhygyfarch's audience would have understood the allusion perfectly well, realising that David's system derived straight from that source. There is nothing like it in the other Welsh saints' *Lives*, save only that of Saint Samson, which is much older than Rhygyfarch's work.

We can also trace David's early asceticism in what we know of Welsh religious life in the sixth century. We have already heard that Gildas wrote critically of monks 'who draw ploughs and dig the earth with mattacks and drive spades into the earth, full of arrogance and pride'. The words are echoed in Rhygyfarch's description five centuries later: the monks 'take the yoke on their shoulders, driving spades and shovels into the earth'.

Although our knowledge of early Welsh monasticism

is slight, evidence from the eleventh century suggests that the harsh monastic way of life had not disappeared entirely from Wales. Gerald of Wales, who was damning of the *clas* at Llanbadarn and of monks in general, was ready to praise the little community on Bardsey Island called Culdees for their devout life. There were also, in Rhygyfarch's own lifetime, hermits who followed the genuinely ascetic life. One such was Caradog, who was buried at St Davids in 1124, and the shell of his shrine still survives in the cathedral. Another was the Englishman Edgar, who left Wales for Ireland and then came to Bardsey.

The *Life of St David* is notable for the numerous mentions of Ireland and Irishmen. That is natural enough considering the position of St Davids at the heart of the so-called Celtic sea lanes. Whether David spent his mature life at St Davids or even in Ceredigion, he would certainly have encountered Irishmen and Irish influences. Sulien's years of education in Ireland would also have contributed to Rhygyfarch's awareness of the importance of Irish influence on David. The number of Irishmen he names is impressive: Patrick, Bairre, Ailbe, Mobi, Aidan, Brendan and Modomnóc are all Irishmen or men who migrated to live in Ireland. It's not surprising that Rhygyfarch claims that 'a third or a quarter of Ireland serves David', although the saint never went there as far as we know. Modomnóc's name appears on an inscription from Llanllŷr, near Talsarn in Ceredigion, made perhaps in the eighth century: the stone marks 'the piece of Ditoc's land which Aon son of Asa Itgen gave to Modomnóc'.

David is named in a number of early Irish chronicles; he also appears in two early lists of martyrs written in Ireland, one in Latin, the other in Irish (we should understand 'martyr' not as one killed for the Faith, but who gave his whole life to it). David is also named in a number of Irish saints' *Lives*: Aidan, Ailbe, Bairre, Declan, Finian, Molua and Senán. The first three also appear in David's *Life*. Ailbe also had a Welsh name, Eilw, and there in a church dedicated to him near Solva, Pembrokeshire, called Llaneilw in Welsh and St Elvis in English.

The high points of Rhygyfarch's narrative are the journey to Jerusalem and the two Synods which demonstrate David's unique status in the British world, and then his death, witnessing to his sanctity and spiritual status. We know that Welshmen made the pilgrimage to Jerusalem in the twelfth century, while others went on crusade about that time: in theory it is perfectly possible that a Welsh priest *might* have journeyed to Jerusalem in the sixth century, but it seems extremely unlikely. Rather, it is more propaganda on the hero's behalf. Rhygyfarch uses the journey to emphasise David's superior status to his fellow-pilgrims Padarn and Teilo. It's no coincidence that Padarn and Teilo's respective spheres of influence border on that of David. Rhygyfarch would have been well aware that the diocese of Menevia had, by his lifetime, taken over control of Teilo's domain, and would reach to the river Dovey, taking in the domain of Padarn.

Propaganda in Rhygyfarch's work reaches its zenith when describing David at the two Synods, Brefi and

Victory. Did they really happen? The Brefi Synod was, of course, supposedly held at Llanddewibrefi: the story of the hillock rising under Dewi's feet is the best-known of all the stories about him. It can be suggested that Rhygyfarch took a folk story about the miraculous rise of the hill (which has a rather artificial look about it from some aspects), and added his own explanation. That is to say, he used the tale as the kernel of an inflated story about David defeating Pelagianism as Germanus had done, and this is the reason for claiming for him the status of archbishop. The existence of the hill and the church crowning it are thus evidence which 'proves' the truth of the story. If, as Rhygyfarch claims, there was one Synod, why not two, without even bothering to name the place where the second one happened, or why it was called, other than to confirm the first. Interestingly, he says that the two Synods meant that 'all the churches of our country received their pattern and rule by Roman authority'. This is a message for the wider Church, claiming that David and his great office were unimpeachably orthodox.

Immediately after the second Synod comes the last of the high points – the death of David at the age of 147. This is not a claim to take seriously: it is part of the legend of Patrick, and since it is a patriarchal age at which to die, like Jacob in the Old Testament, Rhygyfarch treats it as normal. The description of David's passing is a model of how a saint should die: an angel prophesies to him the day of his death, and David welcomes the news, while all others mourn. He calms them with well-known words:

Brethren, be steadfast. Bear to the end the yoke that you have unanimously accepted; and whatever you have seen and heard with me, keep it and fulfil it.

and again:

My brothers, persevere in those things that you have learned from me, and have seen with me; on Tuesday, 1 March, I shall enter the way of the fathers; farewell in the Lord, for I shall go away, we shall not see each other any more in this world.

The Welsh version cleverly digests these two into one well-known paragraph: I quote them here in both languages:

Arglwyddi, frodyr a chwiorydd, byddwch lawen, a chedwch eich ffydd a'ch cred, a gwnewch y pethau bychain a glywsoch ac a welsoch gennyf fi. A minnau a gerddaf y ffordd yr aeth ein tadau.

In English:

Lords, brothers and sisters, be joyful, and keep your faith and belief, and do the little things that you heard and saw me do. And I will tread the path that our fathers took.

The Welsh version is more pleasing, with its plea for joy rather than sorrow, and in its address to both men and women.

After that, we are told, the news reaches all Wales

and Ireland, and everyone is in tears. On the following Sunday David celebrates his last mass, and preaches wonderfully before being taken ill. The people wail and sigh, asking the earth to swallow them up, fire to consume them or the sea to drown them – words which remind us powerfully of Gruffudd ab yr Ynad Coch's great elegy to Llywelyn the Last, or the final speech of Othello, describing the horror and torment which will come with Doomsday. On the appointed day Christ and his angels come to carry David's soul to heaven, and the monks bury his body in his monastery.

In a more personal final paragraph, Rhygyfarch expresses his regret that he is too weak a vessel to convey all the glory of his subject. He refers, as we have already seen, to his sources, 'the most ancient records of our country … which have survived the destruction of insects and the havoc of the years.' We know that all the St Davids library of medieval manuscripts was destroyed by the Reformers, but there is no reason to doubt their existence, at least in part, in Rhygyfarch's time, whatever the devastations wrought by the Vikings. Then comes David's genealogy, followed by the three prayers for mass of his feast day.

We move now from Rhygyfarch's story back to his reasons for writing it, and when it was written. Scholars have suggested a number of dates, from 1081 to 1095–6. A choice of date must depend on our explanation of Rhygyfarch's reasons for writing, and the nature of his audience. That also allows for varying explanations. One possible audience existed within Wales: Church clergy and officials, perhaps especially in Glamorgan, where power was moving from Llantwit Major and Llancarfan to Llandaff. Rhygyfarch would have been keen to persuade them that David was Wales's principal saint, and St Davids his centre of influence. Another audience consisted of Church authorities in England, and royal advisers to the king. They needed to be persuaded of the elevated status of David and the see's claim to metropolitan status as the archbishopric of Wales. Rhygyfarch was naturally identifying himself as David's follower, but he writes as one concerned with Church politics.

Rhygyfarch's aims were not foolish, although the realpolitik of the age was bound to win in the end. There were diocesan problems within Wales, and archiepiscopal problems in England. St Davids had been involved in a struggle with Llandaff for control of the lands of Llandeilo; St Davids won, ensuring that Gower and the Tywi valley were within its boundaries. Boundary problems would also develop between St Davids and the new Norman diocese of St Asaph. Doubtless Rhygyfarch would have heard about the dispute between the archbishoprics of Canterbury and York which began in 1080. St Davids's own struggle to gain (Rhygyfarch would have said 'regain') archiepiscopal status would last from 1115 until 1203, surely fuelled by Rhygyfarch's remarkable book. It's now time to turn to that long battle, which among other things ensured the continuing afterlife of David centuries after his death.

4

The Struggle
for the Archbishopric

The struggle for the archbishopric of St Davids was truly remarkable, part of the greater struggle for the continued political existence of Wales. It involved popes, archbishops of Canterbury, kings of England, princes of Wales, bishops of St Davids, and their clerics. It also involved one of the most remarkable men of his age. Gerald of Wales (c.1146–1223) not only compiled much of the evidence for the struggle, but for decades was personally involved, and probably knew more of the participants than did any other man.

But we must understand from the beginning what was, and is, the office of archbishop. Above all, it is an office, not an order of clergy. There are three orders of clergy: deacon, priest and bishop. There are a host of church *offices*: archdeacon, rector, vicar, curate and so on, but they are not an *order*. An archbishop holds an office, and governs a province, namely a number of dioceses. In the medieval Church an archbishop was answerable only to the pope and his highest representatives. What was the situation in Wales before the Normans came?

The evidence, of course, is skimpy. Welsh clergy certainly believed that St Davids *had* been an archbishopric at one time. There was some fragment of truth in the tale that Saint Samson, when he moved from Wales to Brittany in the sixth century, took with him the *pallium* of St Davids, the mantle which demonstrated that its wearer was an archbishop and his diocese an archbishopric. Samson was a Welshman, somewhat older than David, who had lived *c.*485 to 565. He certainly went to Brittany, and the legend grew that he had founded the cathedral of Dol-de-Bretagne. It's true that Dol did become an archbishopric for a time, but that had been due to two ninth-century kings of Brittany, not to Samson. Moreover, the dates don't fit: Samson probably died nearly thirty years before David. Had the latter really been an archbishop, Samson could hardly have taken the symbol of privilege with him to Brittany.

There are later crumbs of evidence. The *Annales Cambriae* say that Elfoddw, who died in 809, had been archbishop of Gwynedd. Asser claims that his relative, Nobis, had been 'archbishop' of Menevia before being driven from there by Hyfaidd, a violent king of Dyfed. Asser is even described as 'archbishop of the Island of Britain', an extraordinary statement, but lacking any truth whatsoever. This is enough to show that the Welsh knew of the title before Rhygyfarch's time, but those men who may have held it certainly had no status as supreme bishop of Wales, let alone of the island of Britain. It is, however, likely that at one time the bishop of St Davids had authority over a number of local bishops. This would explain the strength of the claims made for St Davids, given that by the eleventh century it had taken over Llandeilo Fawr, once a bishop's seat, and controlled Glasbury in mid Wales, where there had been bishops for several generations.

By Rhygyfarch's lifetime there was certainly a memory of some kind of archiepiscopal status, but the holders of the bishopric had too many worries – not least staying alive – to think of resurrecting the title for themselves. But Rhygyfarch knew what had happened in England after 1066. Within nine years, only one English bishop remained – in Worcester – and when he died there was no thought of an English replacement. That would probably be the fate of the three Welsh bishoprics, which would certainly be placed under Canterbury's control.

It must be understood that Rhygyfarch was no shrinking scholar shut away from the world. He had seen the Normans raping, looting and killing their way through Ceredigion in 1073, 1074 and again in 1094. His powerful Latin 'Elegy' describes their dreadful behaviour at length, of which this is only a sample:

Norman word, heart and deed crush laymen and priests without distinction: one filthy Norman enslaves a hundred people... they are wounded, condemned, enslaved...

In the face of the Norman menace, it was Rhygyfarch who fired the opening salvo in the battle for the archbishopric through his portrait of David, insisting that David had been raised to the status of archbishop not only by the patriarch of Jerusalem but by the multitude at the Synod of Brefi. It's true that Rhygyfarch's father, Sulien, had not claimed the status for himself, although he may have dreamed of it. But, by 1100, as Rhygyfarch's 'Elegy' shows, and, as we know from many sources, Welsh national feeling was growing apace.

Meanwhile, there was a fierce dispute in England between the archbishoprics of Canterbury and York: the former was determined to secure its primacy over all Britain, resulting in the downgrading of York. Thanks to the support of the pope, York won this struggle despite the opposition of Henry I. Canterbury, however, had a much larger number of dioceses under its rule so that, although York kept its status, it was never superior to Canterbury, but accepted its seniority.

This struggle was at its height when the Normans seized the chance to gain control of a Welsh bishopric. Bangor was vacant when Hugh of Chester briefly seized control of Anglesey and Snowdonia, and he secured the appointment of the outsider Hervé as bishop, and since Canterbury was vacant, the archbishop of York consecrated him as the first ever foreign bishop of a Welsh see. But in 1094, Gruffudd ap Cynan drove the Normans out of Gwynedd, and Hervé had to flee, leaving the see vacant for years. The Normans seized the next opportunity in the south, appointing Urban as bishop of Glamorgan (Llandaff) in 1106, with Anselm of Canterbury consecrating him and ensuring an oath of obedience from the new bishop. St Davids was surely the greatest prize, since its diocese embraced virtually half of the Welsh peninsula, and David himself was acknowledged as the foremost Welsh saint.

Sulien had been succeeded at St Davids in 1085 by a Welshman with an English name – Wilfred. Since Rhys ap Tewdwr still ruled the south-west, there was no Norman interference. Wilfred held the see for thirty years, the last bishop to hold it with some degree of independence from Norman influence. With the death of Rhys in 1093, the Normans poured into the diocese, reducing Welsh rule to barely a shadow. Wilfred had to compromise with Canterbury to retain the see, and when he died in 1115, a Norman, Bernard, replaced him.

Bernard readily promised obedience to Canterbury and began to reform his diocese with Norman thoroughness. The see was organised into four archdeaconries. Courts were instituted to administer Church law. The priests of St Davids became canons, members of the chapter responsible for administration and the ordering of worship. Bernard took an interest in the history of his diocese: he was responsible for the interment of Saint Caradog in the cathedral, thus adding to its status. He searched for David's remains, but they had vanished with the Vikings.

Despite Bernard's oath of obedience, Rhygyfarch's archiepiscopal dreams had not disappeared. Bernard was a frequent traveller, especially to London but also to France and Rome. In 1119 he asked the pope for his approval of the cult of Saint David, which was granted about 1123, thus giving a great boost to pilgrimage. He took advantage of the death of King Henry I in 1135

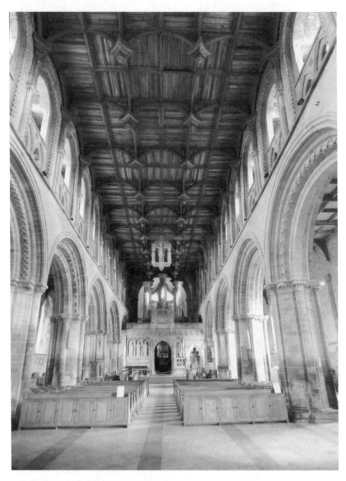

St Davids cathedral: the nave.

and the subsequent anarchy to ask Pope Innocent II to consecrate him as archbishop, while apologising for not having raised the matter earlier. He insisted that, at his consecration in 1115, he should have been raised to the status of archbishop of the oldest and principal diocese in Britain, but he had been denied by Henry I. The pope should understand, he said, that the people of his diocese were different from the English in nationality, language, laws, dress and custom.

It was a good moment to raise the issue of the archbishopric. Not only had Henry died, but Geoffrey of Monmouth had published his extraordinary volume, *The History of the Kings of Britain*, most of whom existed nowhere except in his imagination. However, we should understand that Geoffrey was anxious to paint as glorious and antique a picture of British history as he could. He asserted that Caerleon had been the first archbishopric in Britain, but the title had moved with David to St Davids, a move of which Geoffrey disapproved – Caerleon had been the seat of King Arthur and therefore of greater status!

As well as Bernard's appeal to Innocent II, a letter to Rome survives which – if genuine – was sent by the clergy of St Davids to appeal for the return of the diocese to its ancient status. The letter is full of echoes of Rhygyfarch's *Life*. But, it says, the rights and property of the diocese have been lost through all kinds of unfortunate happenings. St Davids had never been subject to Canterbury in any way. Fear of the Normans explained the failure of Wilfred to nominate his own successor in 1115. It was true that Bernard held the see legally, and the fact of his consecration by the archbishop of Canterbury in no way diminished his status.

Although the letter doesn't mention Rhygyfarch or his book by name, it follows Rhygyfarch's description of how David had been raised to be archbishop. It refers to Patrick leaving the see to evangelise in Ireland, and that a number of David's Irish followers were sent there to preach. It's worth remembering that Daniel ap Sulien, a brother of Rhygyfarch, was a member of the clergy chapter. Bernard did not sign this letter, but he must have given his staff his approval. Certainly, he would have read Rhygyfarch's work during his tenure of office, and thought about it. Even if the letter isn't genuine, it's clear that Bernard was by now ambitious, and had the support of his clergy.

Naturally, any attempt to ensure St Davids's metropolitan status would have infuriated both Canterbury and the English Crown. St Davids would certainly have been supreme in a new province – Wales. In an age when the Church was so politically powerful, a putative 'province of Wales' would have been remarkably significant, even though the province would have been tiny compared with Canterbury. It's hardly surprising, therefore, that both king and archbishop were utterly opposed to any move towards separation: the Welsh Church was to be part of the English Church, thus severely weakening Welsh princely claims to independent rule.

Nevertheless, in 1144, Bernard had gained the support of Owain Gwynedd and his brother Cadwaladr, the sons of Gruffudd ap Cynan. They were trying to secure the unseating of Meurig, the new bishop of Bangor, who had been persuaded to pledge obedience to Theodore, archbishop of Canterbury. The two princes admitted that previously they had withheld their support from Bernard and his claims, but now they were willing to sustain him in all matters. They were happy to discuss, with Anarawd, prince of Deheubarth, what should be done to restore the ancient privileges of Menevia. That support is sufficient evidence of the significance of a potential archbishopric of St Davids – it was no mere clerical matter.

Bernard made a second application for the archbishopric to Pope Lucius II. He was given a diplomatic answer: the pope understood that St Davids had suffered afflictions and losses, but he had not spoken with the bishop himself, nor consulted elderly witnesses and documents. Lucius then died, and was replaced in 1145 by Eugenius III.

Theodore, archbishop of Canterbury, had complained to the new pope about Bernard's claims and behaviour, and Eugenius replied that he had chastised Bernard for his conduct towards Theodore. As for Bernard's allegations, he would hold a meeting in October 1147 to decide on the truth of the status and privileges of St Davids. A copy of the letter was sent to the clergy of St Davids. Indeed, the English historian, Henry of Huntingdon, believed that Bernard had succeeded, but this was a mistake. In 1147 Theodore and Bernard appeared before the pope's representatives in France. It was decided that Bernard had lost his own claim, but the see of St Davids could still argue their case. But that fell away – for a time – when Bernard died in 1148.

It seems extraordinary that Bernard, a Norman who had been a faithful servant of Henry I and his queen, Eleanor of Aquitaine, should have undergone such a dramatic conversion to the cause of his see and his adopted country. Ambition certainly lay at its root: his elevation to an archbishopric would have been a remarkable personal achievement. It would also have had a great effect on St Davids and its status in Wales, making it a potential source of power and influence. No wonder that the Crown and Canterbury were so bitterly hostile. *The Chronicle of the Princes* believed that Bernard deserved praise for his wondrous renown and godly sanctity, and for his labours on behalf of his church.

Theodore moved quickly after Bernard's death to strengthen Canterbury's position. The clergy of St Davids were persuaded to put forward one of their own number as their next bishop. This was David fitz Gerald who, on the face of it, was an ideal candidate. He was already archdeacon of Cardigan. His Cambro-Norman roots were impeccable: he was the son of Nest, daughter of Rhys ap Tewdwr, and therefore of the Welsh princely line. His father was Gerald of Windsor, one of the foremost Norman lords in Deheubarth. David was also uncle to our chief informant about the struggle for the archbishopric, Gerald of Wales.

David was certainly an ideal candidate from Canterbury's point of view. He promised absolute obedience to Theodore, and that he would never raise the issue of the archbishopric. He held the see for twenty-eight years, thus fending off any chance of further dispute. He married and had children without apparently incurring any criticism. He also favoured many of his family with gifts of land and office at the expense of the see. In general he was ineffective, especially compared with Bernard, but one kindness bore fruit: he took his nephew Gerald into his household and ensured his education. The young man went on to study in Paris before returning to further help from his uncle: he was appointed archdeacon of Brecon.

Gerald was now one of the clergy of St Davids, and it is tempting to link him with a new development, but it is unlikely that Gerald would have rebelled against his uncle. In 1176, while David was still bishop, the clergy sent a deputation to London to meet Cardinal Hugh of Sant'Angelo, a papal representative. They argued the case once again for archiepiscopal status, but in vain. It was not the cardinal but the forceful king, Henry II, who put an end to the discussion: he would not permit that in his time, nor give authority in Wales against England by giving the Welsh an archbishop. Two months' later David was dead. Gerald, though barely thirty, was ready for the challenge.

Gerald would prove to be one of the most productive writers – always in Latin – during the Middle Ages. He is best remembered in Wales for his two remarkable and highly-readable books, *The Journey through Wales* and *The Description of Wales*. But these were only two of many, among which are an autobiography, a new version of Rhygyfarch's *Life* and four other saints' *Lives*.

His pen can be waspish indeed: he does not spare his personal enemies, nor the orders of monks.

There's no denying Gerald's egotism: he is his own personal hero before any other. Sometimes he presents himself as Norman, sometimes as fully sympathetic with the Welsh. He is scathing about Bernard's weaknesses, especially for alienating so much Church land to laymen. His uncle David was similarly guilty, but Gerald could hardly savage his own close kin. We have to depend on his work for much of our knowledge of the battle for the archbishopric. He cites numerous letters in favour of his own case which do not survive elsewhere, but he is a credible witness, equally ready to quote – and answer – letters critical of him. We should remember too that he was twice offered other sees, but declined them in order to pursue his goal – St Davids.

So in 1176 the clergy of St Davids nominated Gerald as their choice of bishop. At least, that is what Gerald claims, although one must take the next sentence with a good pinch of salt. He claims that Canterbury and the bishops of England favoured his case. Despite his comparative youth, he certainly was a strong candidate for the see: there is no doubt of his energy, his faith and intellectual ability. He already had experience of administration and travel. He blames Henry II entirely for his failure. Henry had again made himself plain: 'because he is of the family of Rhys ap Gruffudd, prince of south Wales, and almost all the other great men of Wales, the appointment would give new strength to the Welsh.'

Therefore the king chose a monk from Much Wenlock, Peter Leia, as the new bishop, as long as he promised complete obedience to Canterbury. In 1182 Peter began building the new cathedral in great splendour, and held the see until his death in 1198.

All this while Rhys ap Gruffudd had been consolidating Deheubarth until he ruled much of what his grandfather, Rhys ap Tewdwr, had held. He was able to do so thanks to the leeway Henry II allowed him, but he had little influence on episcopal elections to St Davids. By contrast, Owain Gwynedd had had much greater power in Bangor to resist intrusions from outside. Most of Rhys's family and successors were buried at Strata Florida, but he was interred at St Davids, to be joined by two of his many sons, Maredudd, archdeacon of Cardigan, in 1227, and Rhys Gryg in 1234. There were difficulties: Rhys died excommunicate, thanks to the behaviour of his sons towards Bishop Peter. Therefore Rhys's corpse had to be subjected to a solemn lashing before it was buried. The stone effigy on his grave was placed there in the fourteenth century.

*

Gerald swallowed his disappointment, spending a period lecturing in Paris and then with Prince John in Ireland in 1183. In 1188 he escorted Baldwin, archbishop of Canterbury, on his tour of Wales. This enabled Baldwin to celebrate mass in each of the Welsh cathedrals, thus demonstrating his authority over them. Gerald spent the following decade in England, but in

1198 Bishop Peter died, and once more the clergy of St Davids nominated Gerald as their choice for approval by Crown and Canterbury.

This battle was much more bitter than that of 1176. The death of King Richard I in 1199 complicated matters, but it seemed to be Gerald's last chance; he had, after all, been close to John, the new king, during their time in Ireland. But Canterbury was as stubborn as ever. Three times during the years 1198 to 1203 Gerald, no longer a young man, rode and walked to Rome and back, braving robbers, to argue his case before the formidable Pope Innocent III. The latter seemed at first to favour Gerald, who had the support of Llywelyn ab Iorwerth of Gwynedd and other Welsh princes. But, by 1203, the support of the clergy of St Davids was weakening, and the fickle King John had turned against Gerald. Before the end of that year Geoffrey, prior of Llanthony in Gwent, had been consecrated bishop of St Davids.

When Geoffrey died in 1214 the clergy of St Davids turned again to Gerald, but by now he preferred the company of his books. Nearly seventy years old, he could not possibly have mustered the vigour needed to face struggle and disappointment yet again. This did not prevent him from savage criticism of the 'arch-thieves' in St Davids who had deprived him of promotion (as he saw it) in 1203. He took comfort from the fact that Llywelyn ab Iorwerth, one of his supporters, had been able to ensure the appointment of a Welshman to St Davids. King John, in the middle of his struggles with the barons, yielded, and Iorwerth, abbot of Talley, was the new bishop.

St Non's chapel, near St Davids.

St Non's well, just above her chapel.

So with Gerald's death in 1223, just over a century after Rhygyfarch had died, there vanished the dream that St Davids could become an archbishop's seat. True, the ashes were stirred a little in 1284, at which time the bishop was Thomas Bec, founder of the college of priests in Llanddewibrefi. Edward I was touring Wales after his conquest, with John Pecham, archbishop of Canterbury, in his train. Bec tried to insist that Pecham should not come to St Davids because of its metropolitan status, but Pecham threatened to excommunicate him, and Bec yielded.

Perhaps the most important medieval bishop of St Davids after Peter Leia was Henry de Gower (1278?–1347). He built the cathedral's Lady Chapel, the great stone screen and the splendid bishop's palace. He was not interested in raising the debate again, although he was willing to honour David with the title of archbishop when he established a hospital in Swansea in the saint's name in 1332. Alas, it was destroyed by Reformers in 1549.

The dream revived for a moment in the imagination of Owain Glyndŵr, who sought to rule a Greater Wales, reaching to Worcester, with a Church independent of Canterbury. St Davids would certainly have been its metropolitan seat. But it was only realised in 1920 with the disestablishment of the Church of England in Wales. Ironically, the first archbishop was G A Edwards, bishop of St Asaph and a dedicated opponent of disestablishment until seduced by the charm of Lloyd George. St Asaph's had not even been a diocese in Rhygyfarch's time, and the modern office of archbishop is not attached to one diocese, but goes with the appointee.

A historian should beware of asking 'what if?'. But there's a fairly simple answer to the question: what if Gerald had become bishop of St Davids? He would never have succeeded in achieving archiepiscopal status in the face of the Crown and Canterbury's opposition. He would probably have been too busy to write most of the books which he produced in his retirement which secured him such a prominent place among European authors.

5

David's Wealth, David's Pilgrims

It seems contradictory to speak of 'David's wealth' as if we are dealing with this world's treasure. David, like Jesus and his followers, foreswore the secular riches of life, seeking instead to lay up treasure in heaven. He embraced poverty for himself and his monks; life without property was fundamental to their discipline, following the Apostles, imitating Saint Anthony and Saint Benedict, the founders of Christian monasticism.

Yet the monks needed land to establish their community, a place to cultivate for food, a place to live apart from the world. Such lands had to be the gifts of the kings, princes and lords who had possessed them in the first place. Naturally, the donors wanted a return for their valuable gifts, a return which they believed would be in perpetuity. They could hope for both spiritual and secular benefits. Spiritually they expected the monks to pray and say masses for them and their families, especially in the hope of lessening their souls' time in purgatory. But they also expected more tangible benefits. Monks would act as royal clerks, chroniclers and ambassadors. They would act as treasurers of valuables. Some donors might retire to a monastery to assume the monastic habit, receive medical care and die in the odour of sanctity. But there is no indication that donors of land received such benefits in David's own time.

Monasteries and churches could expect more than land by way of gifts. They needed money to build, extend and repair their buildings, they needed relics for their sanctuaries, and those needed to be gilded and bejewelled. Although ninety-nine per cent of the treasures in medieval Welsh churches and monasteries have vanished, Peter Lord has shown that enough remains to give some idea of the wealth that has been lost: alabaster tombs like those that survive in churches from Penmynydd to Cardiff, wooden figures like the mighty Jesse of Abergavenny, the paintings of St Teilo's church, Llandeilo Tal-y-bont, manuscripts like those of Llanbadarn Fawr, the wonderful stained glass of Llanrhaeadr-yng-Nghinmeirch, Clwyd, the gilded altar cross in Monmouth, the candletrees of Llanarmon-yn-Iâl, Clwyd, the exquisitely embroidered cloak at Skenfrith, Monmouthshire, and the oak screens that still survive in some forty Welsh churches, though their colours and carved figures have disappeared.

Of course these treasures belong to much later times than David's. But, although Wales has been poor for much of her history, there were surely treasures in ecclesiastical hands between the age of David and the coming of the Normans. There is enough evidence from Ireland, Anglo-Saxon England and the Continent to show how common were artistic treasures across the

Christian world. We have seen how often the Vikings pillaged Menevia and its sanctuary. What, we may wonder, was the Torque of Cynog that the Lord Rhys stole from its owners and hid in his Dinefwr stronghold? A Welsh treasure that still survives is the *Teilo Gospels*, traded away to Lichfield a thousand years ago, now called the *St Chad* or *Lichfield Gospels*.

Despite the Vikings and other raiders, relics of Saint David re-emerged or were invented by 1326, because we know that tenants working the bishop's lands had to follow the saint's relics on special occasions, either in peace or war. These would have been carried in special containers, reliquaries, made of ornamented metal. *The Black Book of St Davids* was compiled in 1326, listing all the diocesan estates. They stretched across Pembrokeshire and Ceredigion as far as the river Dovey in the north, and to the Welsh border with England in the east, and from Brecon down to Swansea and Gower. Episcopal income came not only from land rents but from fairs, markets, mills and numerous financial duties.

Despite the details of the *Black Book*, it doesn't seem possible to estimate the actual acreage of the diocesan lands. Much of the land in Ceredigion and the Tywi valley was still organised in *gwelyau*, clan holdings by groups of relatives. Most of the rest was held by more usual arrangements. The book lists hundreds of tenants by name, many of whom are interesting and unusual: Henry Peacock and Tankard stand out from the English names, while Welsh names can be translated into English as John the Welshman, Iorwerth the Hunchback,

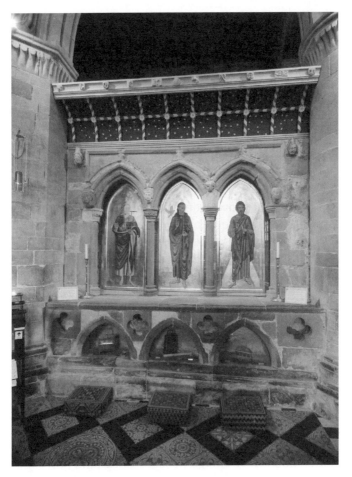

The restored shrine of Saint David, in the cathedral.

Isabella the Fox and Cadwgan the Harper. There are old Welsh forms, like Gwasfihangel (servant of Saint Michael) and Adda ap Gwasdewi (Adam, the son of the servant of Saint David). Besides the complexity of rents and duties, land measurements are ambiguous and prevent us from understanding how much land there was, and what income was earned from it.

Who had given all these lands to the bishops of St Davids? We have seen already that Rhys ap Tewdwr gave the whole of Pebidiog in 1081 in acknowledgement of Sulien's help. Few documents survive, but we can gather that Rhys ap Tewdwr's descendants, especially Rhys ap Gruffudd and his sons, all gave land to the bishops of St Davids, as well as to the abbeys of St Dogmaels, Talley and Strata Florida, and the nunnery at Llanllŷr. Names like Morfa Esgob and Fforest-yr-esgob in Ceredigion show how broad were these acres (esgob = bishop).

Gerald of Wales insisted that bishops Bernard and David fitz Gerald had alienated much land to the Norman lords, both in Pembrokeshire between Milford and Pebidiog, Trallong in Brecknockshire and Oystermouth between Swansea and Gower. Worse than that, says Gerald: 'David fitz Gerald made no effort to recover lands lost earlier, but gave what was left to the sons of the great men of the land.' Despite these losses the bishopric still held much land, although it could not compare with the great sees of England.

As for the relics, Bishop Bernard had searched in vain for them after the Viking raids. But some time during the period 1260–75, one John de Gamages, prior of Ewenny in Glamorgan, had dreamed of the location of David's bones, after they had been lost for more than 160 years. It's intriguing that an Englishman should have had this dream: clearly the loss of the relics was well known. John certainly knew that St Davids owned two pieces of land which had once belonged to the abbey of Gloucester, because Ewenny was a subordinate priory to the abbey. We may guess that John might have hoped to regain the lands for his order in exchange for the bones of David. The result was that Thomas Wallensis ('of Wales'), bishop of St Davids, in 1275 began to build a stone shrine for the bones, the same shrine which has recently been restored. When Edward I came to St Davids he took away the skull, and among his goods at the time of his death was 'David's arm'. The remaining bones (whoever's they may really have been) were the object of pilgrimage for centuries, and would have been taken regularly on tour in the diocese.

*

Other than the diocesan lands, the main source of income was the pilgrim industry. Alas, no records survive to tell us how many pilgrims came annually to St Davids, nor how much came in by way of donations, and no doubt the purchase of souvenirs. We know that William I, Henry II, Edward I and Richard II all gave gifts to David's sanctuary. They may not have been especially valuable, since kings were expected to give to every one of the many shrines they would visit while travelling. But the very size of the cathedral and palace built respectively by bishops Peter Leia and Henry de Gower, suggests that the income must have been substantial. One result of St Davids's fame was its inclusion on the Hereford Mappa Mundi: the only other Welsh places named are Caernarfon and Conwy.

Pilgrims would travel to St Davids for many reasons. The original purpose was to make a sacrificial journey involving courage, effort and expense so as to pray to the saint for the souls of the pilgrim and his or her family and, in particular, to lessen the pains of purgatory after death. But motives would often be mixed: curiosity about the world beyond one's parish was one, while another was simply to have a holiday (holy-day). An English drama of the sixteenth century lists many places associated with the saints of Europe visited by pilgrims, including 'St Davy's'. Some places of pilgrimage were noteworthy for their images of the Rood, the Cross of Christ, like those at Chester, Brecon and Llangynwyd. There was no special cross associated with St Davids as far as is known: the sanctuary was at the centre of devotion, and pilgrims could put in their hands to touch the saint's supposed bones.

The whole landscape around St Davids was sacred to pilgrims. Apart from the glories of the cathedral and the shrines of David and Caradog, there were the chapels of Justinian, Non, Patrick and Gwrhyd within two miles. There were chapels of David and Dywan on Ramsey Island. Then there were all the holy wells in the area and beyond, most of which have now vanished. As well as David and the other more local saints, there was a special devotion in the fifteenth century, if not

The reliquary of Saint Non, Dirinon, Brittany

sooner, to the Virgin Mary. There was a Lady's Well near St Mary's College (now the restaurant), and there are poems to Our Lady of St Davids by Welsh poets.

Only fragments of evidence remain to tell us how much the pilgrims contributed to the church. In 1490 the chapels of Justinian, Non and Gwrhyd received £11, which went to the cathedral's funds. A procession in the same year, with David's bones visiting Brecon, Gower and the south of the diocese, brought in £5.15.0. A similar sum was the fruit of another procession in 1492 through Ystrad Tywi, Brecknockshire, and the south of the diocese. It was claimed that donations to St Patrick's chapel were so generous that they were weighed, not counted.

Not all pilgrims succeeded in reaching their goal, and many failed to return home thanks to the dangers of medieval travel. This is clear from the graveyard of the ruined church of Llanfihangel Abercywyn, where the river Cywyn flows into the Taff, south-east of St Clears and north of Laugharne. There are six medieval gravestones (rare enough in any Welsh churchyard), four of which show figures of pilgrims. According to tradition they were on their way to Santiago de Compostela in Galicia, Spain, but St Davids could perhaps have been their objective. They may have died, possibly drowned, some time in the thirteenth century. The stones are more primitive in form that the gravestone of a pilgrim in Saint Tyfodwg's church, Glyn Ogwr, Glamorgan. That stone has carved into it a staff, keys and scallop shell, all typical of the medieval pilgrim.

The pilgrim tradition was so strong that medieval Welsh poets felt able to make fun of the custom. Thus Dafydd ap Gwilym composed his splendid poem 'A Girl's Pilgrimage'. The poet claims to have died of love, rejected by a stubborn girl in Anglesey. Her penance is to go on a pilgrimage to St Davids to seek absolution. She will go, says Dafydd, 'in the name of Non and Dewi', and he prays that all the rivers on the way will allow her easy passage.

More serious is a poem by Lewis Glyn Cothi describing the visit of his lady patron Erdudfyl, daughter of Cadwgan, to the chapel of Non and to St Davids cathedral. Its charm is almost, but not entirely, lost in translation:

Erdudfyl on Sunday comes
To pray to the one true God;
She rests her body at Non's chapel,
She lays her head by the well,
She raises her hands joyfully,
Worshipping the fair image,
Lighting great yellow candles,
Placing them on the altar;
Thence she goes to David's church,
Offering, while kissing the saint,
Red candles and silver to him.

The Reformation brought an end to pilgrimages to St Davids for several centuries. It seems to have been revived only in the twentieth century: members of the Society of St David at Lampeter made a pilgrimage there in 1926, and again in 1928. Today tens of thousands of people visit the cathedral every year, yet only a minority would describe themselves as pilgrims in the traditional sense of the word.

Note: Saint David's Wells

Space will not permit more than a few words about holy wells bearing Saint David's name, although they would all have been objects of pilgrimage at some stage. Francis Jones made a survey of all the holy wells in Wales in 1954, and counted 437, some bearing the names of individual saints. There were thirty-two David wells, all in south Wales, and eighteen of those in Pembrokeshire. That is certainly a larger number than for any other Welsh saint.

So large was the total that it was impossible for one individual to visit every one. Much of the research had to be done with books and maps. Jones recognised that some wells had disappeared by the time of his research, and others have since vanished thanks to building work, road widening and general neglect. Of the several David wells known to me, none compares with St Divy's well near Dirinon, Brittany (see chapter 8) or the St David's well at Ballinaslaney, Oylegate, County Wexford, Ireland (see page 117).

St Divy's well,
near Dirinon

6

Saint David in Church Worship to 1560

How would David and his brother monks worship God in their monastery? Although we have no relevant manuscripts from Wales for the period, we can be sure of the basics. Since virtually the foundation of Christendom, some form of mass has been at the centre of Christian worship. The services of the early Church in Jerusalem, Antioch, Rome and Alexandria obeyed Christ's command to bless bread and wine and share it among those present.

These services would at first have been in Greek and Aramaic, the mother tongue of Jesus, and they would have kept elements of worship in the temple at Jerusalem, especially the chanting of Psalms. Latin quickly developed as the language of worship in Rome and the West, with Latin translations of texts of the Bible and the liturgy spreading through Gaul, Britain and Ireland. David, like every bishop, abbot and priest, would have used appropriate manuscripts for daily church worship. The monastic order of life followed by David meant that worship and work were one. Rhygyfarch's reference to chanting the Psalms is quite appropriate. His assertion that David learnt by heart the Psalms, the Biblical readings for the Church year, and the liturgy is surely true.

In the cathedrals and monasteries of medieval Europe, communities of monks and clergy would recite the daily round of services as well as mass. The inspiration for this lay in Psalm 119: 'Seven times a day I will praise you, because of the justice of your judgements.' These services were, in fact, eight in number: matins, lauds, prime, terce, sext, none, vespers and compline. David was certainly dead before this rota was formalised, but it would have been familiar to Rhygyfarch.

With the passage of time, priests in the churches of south Wales, and some in Ireland, would have named David regularly in their Sunday worship, and especially so on 1 March. His name would have been included in the mass with other saints. The intention was to beseech them to intercede in heaven to God, asking for blessing and pardon for the congregation.

On 1 March in any church dedicated in David's name, and in a growing number of other churches, mass would contain the three particular prayers prescribed for David's festival. They are the collect, the secret, and the post-Communion prayers. They appear in the manuscripts of David's *Life* and in other documents. We don't know when they were composed, but they are certainly older than the year 1100.

During the high Middle Ages, David was given increasing attention in the churches of Britain. From 1050 onwards, 1 March was a special day of commemoration of 'David, archbishop of Britain'. His name appears in a growing number of prayer books in Wales, Ireland and the west of England. In 1398 churches throughout the archdiocese of Canterbury were ordered to commemorate St David's Day.

Thus David would be remembered on his feast day with a series of readings, prayers and chants for all the day's services, including mass. We know this despite the destruction of all the medieval service books of St Davids itself; some in 1538 by the Reformer Bishop Barlow, others in 1550, 1568 and 1571. On the last occasion, the sexton Elis ap Hywel tried to hide the cathedral's 'masse books, hympnalls, grailes, antiphoners and suchlike', but they were torn into shreds before his eyes. Similar vandalism took place across Britain.

However, a handful of books survive to give us a good idea of the order of services for the feast of Saint David. The most important of these only came to light in 1969, when a private owner sold it at a Sotheby's auction and it was bought by the National Library of Wales. It was given the name *The Penpont Antiphonal*, since it had lain unrecognised for centuries at the Penpont mansion in the Brecon Beacons National Park, between Brecon and Sennybridge. An antiphonal is a large volume containing chants and texts for the liturgical year, to be sung by a double choir. The manuscript was written in the St Davids diocese during the fourteenth century.

The Penpont Antiphonal is one of the great treasures of the National Library, though little known in Wales. It's the only survivor in Wales of a class of manuscript of which there were once scores, if not hundreds. Barely twenty survive in Britain. It is unique because not only does it include the prayers and readings for St David's Day, but also the music for the chants, composed in the thirteenth century.

The Penpont Antiphonal is in two parts. The *Temporale* includes services for the Church year from Christmas onwards. The *Sanctorale* contains services for the principal saints' days, from Saint Andrew in Advent to Saint Catherine of Alexandria on 25 November. David is the only British saint to have his own festival services included. Others are mentioned – Swithin, King Edmund, Thomas of Canterbury – but only so that they can be mentioned on their own festival days.

The texts for the saints' festivals, including Saint David, are woven from the Bible, appropriate prayers, and incidents from the individual's life, especially miracles and, in David's case, his ascetic way of life and his triumph over the Pelagian heresy. Professor Owain Tudor Edwards, who has published a study of the text, judges that the music is a century older than the manuscript. The composer, the compiler of the texts, and the scribe are all unknown to us. But the volume shows beyond doubt that the complete Catholic cycle of worship for the whole year was performed in Wales, and not only at St Davids.

The prayers and readings for St David's Day can be found in a few other medieval manuscripts: one at the Bibliothèque nationale de France in Paris is worthy of attention. It includes miniature images of David and scenes from Rhygyfarch's *Life,* including Gildas struck dumb by the presence of the pregnant Saint Non in the

A page from *The Penpont Antiphonal.*

church, David being ordained priest, and healing the eyes of his teacher, Paulinus.

*

All this ended in Britain with the Protestant Reformation, although destroying it took a great deal of effort and much vandalism. St Davids struggled between 1538 and 1571 to preserve its treasures, but in vain. Not everyone abandoned Catholic tradition and practice after Elizabeth I's enthronement in 1558. Some Welsh men and women escaped to the Continent to become or remain Catholic priests or to enter a convent. The men would often return to minister in secret to small groups and families; some paid with their lives for their faith and courage. We know that some holy places, especially Holywell, Flintshire, still attracted frequent visitors. Erasmus Saunders, writing in 1721, tells us that the common people of Pembrokeshire still used prayers to the Virgin Mary and the saints. Two carols to Mary were passed down in a New Quay family for centuries, the only survivors of many once popular.

As late as 1670 Father John Hughes prepared a book of devotions for his little flock in Wales, *Allwydd neu Agoriad Paradwys i'r Cymru* [A Key to Open Paradise to the Welsh], attributed to a press in Liège, but probably printed in London. It lists many Welsh saints, with David foremost in their midst. David's name recurs in English missals for Catholics, and there was never a danger of his disappearance from their worship, where the cult of the saints still lives on.

7

David and the Poets of Wales

The golden age of Welsh prose was the period between 1150 and 1400: this was the time of the *Four Branches of the Mabinogi*, *Culhwch and Olwen*, *The Laws of Hywel Dda*, and many translated texts. It was also a golden age for Latin texts by Welsh authors, including the works of Gerald of Wales, Geoffrey of Monmouth, Walter Map, and the saints' *Lives* by Rhygyfarch, Lifris, and other anonymous authors. Extend the dates from 1100 to 1600, and it was the great age of Welsh poetry. Praising the princes, and their successors as leaders of Welsh society, the *uchelwyr*, was fundamental to the work of the poets, though love of women and of nature also figure, as does Christian faith. Of these poems, the most important for our purpose is the ode to Saint David composed by Gwynfardd Brycheiniog in the twelfth century. This major work deserves far more discussion than is possible here.

Morfydd Owen, editor of Gwynfardd's ode, believes it was originally composed for an audience of clergy and laymen meeting at Llanddewibrefi, perhaps between 1170 and 1180, in the presence of the Lord

Rhys, ruler of Deheubarth. All present would have been familiar, at least to some extent, with the difficult poetic rhetoric of the period. They would also have been completely familiar with the traditional knowledge of David's life. It is a substantial poem, 296 lines long, by a poet well versed in the story of David. Although Rhygyfarch's Latin work had not yet been rendered into Welsh, Gwynfardd knew the text well, as well as other traditions apparently not known to Rhygyfarch.

Gwynfardd tells us his intention is:

To sing to great David, and praise the saints

David has been to Jerusalem, the poet says: he raised the boy Magna from death to life, and did many other miracles. Deheubarth, Pebidiog and a share of Ireland are all David's. All who love David are honest, peaceable; they love mass and the poor. Gwynfardd names Sant, Non and Paulinus from the *Life*; David's lands reach from Caron to the 'fair shining river' Tywi, from Llyn Du near Strata Florida to the river Twrch, and all is ruled by the Lord Rhys.

The Synod of Brefi and David's status are fundamental; seven thousand and seven score men were at the Synod. The saints came from Anjou and Brittany, England and Wessex, from the North (of Britain), the Isle of Man and the Western Isles, from Powys, Ireland, Anglesey, Gwynedd, Devon, Kent, Brecknock and Maelienydd.

Gwynfardd mentions traditions that are not in the *Life*: David went to Rome, he tells us, where the saint was struck a blow by a wretched woman. He mentions:

David's two oxen, a glorious pair…

These are the oxen of Bannog, characters in the Welsh folklore of Ceredigion. Among their legendary feats was ploughing a dyke marking the boundary between Upper Caron and Lower Caron, which is still visible today. According to Gwynfardd, the oxen carried three of David's treasures to Brycheiniog, the poet's own land. One of them was the bell, Bangu, which is remembered in Glascwm, Radnorshire, an early church of David. As well as praising David and the Synod of Brefi, Gwynfardd fires his audience with enthusiasm for David. Then he names David's churches: the cathedral, Abergwili, Bangor Teifi, Cregrina, Garthbrengi, Glascwm, Henfynyw, Henllan Teifi, Llannarth, Llanddewibrefi, Llanddewi Ystrad Enni, Llan-faes (Brecon), Llangadog, Llangyfelach, Llywel, Llanycrwys, Maenordeifi, Meidrim and Trallong. This is more than enough to demonstrate the wide reach of the influence of the cult of David by the twelfth century and earlier. Morfydd Owen has shown the importance of the ode's references to the nature of the early Welsh churches. Gwynfardd mentions the privilege and protection of Llanddewibrefi, 'the tribal nature of the community, the fame of the relics, and the congregation'.

Other poets of the period name David of course, but not in great detail: he is mentioned by the brothers

Meilyr and Einion ap Gwalchmai, by Cynddelw Brydydd Mawr and Llywelyn Fardd.

During the fourteenth century the *cywydd* came to the fore as the preferred poetic form of the poets of the *uchelwyr*. It is simpler than the odes of the poets of the princes, consisting of lines of seven syllables in rhyming couplets, with *cynghanedd* (assonance and alliteration) in every line. A number of these poets of the fourteenth to the sixteenth century sang poems to Saint David: Iolo Goch, Ieuan ap Rhydderch, Lewis Glyn Cothi, Dafydd Llwyd of Mathafarn, Rhisiart ap Rhys and Tomos ab Ieuan ap Rhys. Two of the poems stand out from the rest.

The first is Iolo Goch's *cywydd* to David. He depends, as do the others, on Rhygyfarch's work. But there is a more personal note to Iolo's poem. He would have liked to make a pilgrimage 'to the place where Christ was crucified', but old age, as was inevitable, has overtaken him. But:

> I know where I wish to be…
> in David's land, Menevia

where he will find great music, in the place we all know is as good as Rome. He praises David for relaxing the fierce discipline of Lent (wishful thinking for which David should hardly be credited). He tells of Gwydre and Odrud, two sinners who had been turned into wolves, but David restored them to human form.

Iolo was impressed by the thought of David's death:

On Tuesday in March in the grave
He lay down to die.
There were at his graveside, a worthy end,
Fine poets singing Gloria.

Iolo ends by assuring his hearers that a year and three days would be needed to write the whole history of David in a book.

The other impressive poem is the work of Ieuan ap Rhydderch, a generation later than Iolo. Again, the poem is based on Rhygyfarch's text: Patrick, Sant and Non, Gildas, David's education with Paulinus, his visit to Bath, and to Jerusalem with Padarn and Teilo. He describes the setting in *Vallis Rosina* and the resurrection of Magna. A paragraph is devoted to the Synod of Brefi, with its 'seven score thousand and seven thousand', and David's voice as audible as a bell in fair St Dogmaels. Two paragraphs describe the cathedral, which is like the temple King David sought to build in Jerusalem, playing on the double reference to David. Apart from Rhygyfarch's text, Ieuan refers to other matters. For example, he elaborates on David's visit to Rome where, on his arrival, the church bells rang out in his honour without human involvement.

Lewis Glyn Cothi is the only poet to have written two poems to David. The first is a précis of Rhygyfarch's *Life*, in which he describes the régime at the saint's monastery:

He took bread and watercress,
The water of cold rivers,

> Horsehair was his only dress,
> Penitent at the fountain's edge.

The second poem focuses on David's cult in the district of Elfael (in Radnorshire), naming the churches of Glascwm, Cregrina, Colfa and Rhulen. The poem's purpose is to call on the poet to make peace between two quarrelsome groups within a family:

> To your parishes, fair David…
> There came long hurt and plague,
> God knows, between kinsfolk.
> David, eagle of the east,
> Make peace between them.

Thirty-nine of Lewis Glyn Cothi's numerous poems name David in passing. He was not the only poet to do so. 'By David' (Welsh *Myn Dewi*) is a frequent exclamation or oath, and the saint is used as a moral example for later men. Thus Dafydd Epynt, praising John Morgan, bishop of St Davids (1496–1504), claims that he is a brother and kinsman to David. Guto'r Glyn, in his elegy for Benet, parson of Corwen, wishes that he could bring back David to resurrect the dead man.

With the strangulation of Catholic Wales by the Reformation, and the slow death of the poetry of the *uchelwyr* after 1600, David ceased to be of interest to Welsh poets for several centuries. We shall, however, see in the next chapter how ballad-singers and others kept David alive in English verse. It was only with the rise in the popularity of celebrating St David's Day in Wales that the saint returned to the Welsh poetic repertoire. Much doggerel was recited at St David's Day dinners and printed in the nineteenth-century local press.

The first modern generation of major Welsh poets – W J Gruffydd, R Williams Parry and T H Parry-Williams – had little interest in Saint David. But the next generation – Saunders Lewis, Gwenallt Jones and Waldo Williams – were all men of faith, open to religious subjects. 'Saint David's Last Sermon' is a meditation typical of Saunders Lewis. The relaxed measure enabled him to include the famous last words almost unaltered. Gwenallt Jones was going through a crisis of faith when he wrote the poem beginning 'There is no boundary between the two worlds in the Church'. He saw David as his contemporary:

I saw David tramping from shire to shire like God's gipsy,
And the Gospel and Altar with him in his caravan,
Coming to us in the colleges and schools
To show us the whole purpose of learning.
He descended into the mine with the colliers
To shine his lamp on the coalface.

Waldo's poem to St Davids is more complex and ambitious than the work of Saunders Lewis and Gwenallt. As a Quaker, he was suspicious of the architectural wonder of the cathedral. His poem, 'St David's Day' is difficult, but rewords the original discipline of David in vivid Welsh:

Contemporary figure of Saint David by Frederick Mancini, Llanddewibrefi church.

Figure of Saint David by John Petts, Briton Ferry Roman Catholic Church.

Photograph: Anthony Bentham

With the rope across his back and under his armpits
The saint hauled the plough, and ripped the earth.
Barefoot he trod the stones then, and found
The furrow under his foot a lasting bliss.

He considers the fruit of David's labour:

He sowed the seed that became after his death
The bread of Christ to thousands of privileged tables.

Other people used the Welsh-language *Life* for

musical and poetic purposes. W S Gwynn Williams arranged a St David's Day composition for a women's choir, and it was broadcast in March 1942. Aneirin Talfan Davies wrote the text for composer Arwel Hughes's cantata, *Dewi Sant*. When the poet-artist-professor Moelwyn Merchant arranged a festival of the arts in Llanddewibrefi in 1976, he and Norah Isaac prepared an English text to be the framework for a church service there.

*

The vandalism of the centuries destroyed ninety-nine per cent of the wealth of paintings, stained glass, carvings and ornaments of the medieval Church in Britain, leaving churches and cathedrals looking like barns. Every portrait of David was lost, apart from a handful of miniatures in manuscripts. Only in the twentieth century did public statues of David reappear, in Cardiff City Hall and in Llanddewibrefi church. The best modern image of David known to me is the work of John Petts in Briton Ferry Catholic church. Fortunately, things are different in Brittany, as the next chapter will show.

8

Saint David
in Brittany and Ireland

It's surprising how the early saints got around, alive or dead, if we believe some of what we are told. Saint James the Great in Galicia, Spain? Saint George the Greek in England? Saint Andrew the Apostle in Scotland? Joseph of Arimathea in Glastonbury? Wales welcomed a few lesser outsiders: Quriaqos of Asia Minor became Curig in mid and north Wales, while the cult of Ursula and her eleven thousand virgins reached Llangwyryfon in mid Ceredigion, thanks to a misunderstood place name! Irish saints certainly travelled, not only to Wales but to Scotland, England and central Europe.

So we may ask whether David travelled beyond south-west Wales? There are certainly churches founded in his name in England, Cornwall, Brittany and Ireland, but does that prove anything about David himself? Only that his cult reached those places. A number of Welsh saints are said to have travelled to Brittany via Cornwall, including Samson, Gildas and Illtud, but the evidence is flimsy, though the journeys are reasonable. Who therefore travelled – the saints themselves, or their followers?

The answer is surely 'some of both'. For Brittany, we may turn first to Non, David's mother-figure. She is the only Welsh female saint with a cult in both Cornwall and Brittany. There is only one Non church in Brittany, but it is most remarkable. Dirinon is a village south of Landerneau, which is a substantial town east of Brest. The usual interpretation of the place name is 'the oak trees of Non', although some sceptical scholars suggest that the cult of Non was invented, so to speak, from the place name. Non's church in Dirinon, although not mentioned in the area's *Michelin Guide*, is a splendid medieval building within a substantial enclosure, and the country round about echoes to her name, though there is nothing early (say pre-1300) to indicate her presence in Brittany.

Non is not mentioned in early Breton documents, but David is named as 'Sanctus Devius' in the *Life of St. Paul Aurelian*, written in 884; this is the document which called him *Aquaticus*, the water drinker. The Breton version of David's name is *Divy*, which obviously derives from the *Dewi* of south-west Wales, and, as we shall see, there are many Breton dedications to him.

Above the west door of Dirinon church is a medieval statue of Non reading a book. On the wall inside the church porch are two rows of slender stone statues – the twelve Apostles. Inside the church itself are painted representations of saints the whole length of the nave ceiling, male on the north side, female on the south, led by Non, who faces David. On one of the nave pillars is a fine medieval statue of David, next to one of Saint Antony of Egypt. In a glass case is a fine silver reliquary, reputedly containing some of Non's bones.

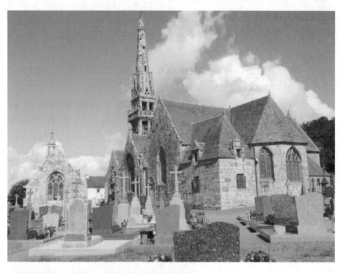

Dirinon church, Brittany, with Non's grave-chapel to the left.

Photograph: Chris Davison

Wooden carving of Saint Non in her chapel, Dirinon. Date unknown.

Figure of Non lying on her tomb: grave-chapel, Dirinon. Late medieval?

St Non's well, near Dirinon.

Saint David at the Synod of Brefi: chancel roof, St Divy's church, Saint-Divy, near Landerneau.

Outside, on the south side of the church, is a medieval chapel containing the tomb of Saint Non.

In 2015, when I was preparing the original Welsh text of this book, I couldn't gain access to the chapel on my visit to Dirinon, despite enquiries at the village *tabac* and the mayor's office, and speaking to the parish priest, who denied all knowledge of any way to open the chapel. I therefore had to rely on the splendid 1999 Breton-French volume *Buez Santez Nonn: mystère breton: vie de Sainte Nonne,* now out of print (see the Bibliography under the name of Bernard Tanguy). In 2016 my brother-in-law Chris Davison tracked down the church's caretaker, Mme Yvonne Malléjac, who proved most kind and helpful. We were thus able to spend time in the chapel. (Until 1939 Non's *Life* is said to have been read annually in public in the Breton original in the church.)

The building needs money spent on it to supplement that already spent on restoring Non's tomb. Her life-size effigy, carved some time during the years 1300 to 1450, lies at full length, her feet resting on an extraordinary lion-like beast apparently engaged in swallowing an octopus! The carving of her face reflects a lovely calm. The chapel also has a wooden wall-sculpture of Non, and portrays her in rather gaudy stained glass in the east window.

That is not all. A mile south of Dirinon, on a back road, is Non's well with another statue, and less than half-a-mile away is St David's well. These are both easily found, but I failed to locate two other stones, known as Divy's cradle and Non's stone. Not far away is a locked chapel of St David, with little in the way of visible art.

David or Divy's own parish church is in the village of Saint-Divy, west of Landerneau. There is a problem in following Divy through Brittany, and that is because of the popularity of another saint, *Yves* in French but *Ivi* in Breton, so in some cases Saint-Ivi and Saint-Divy may have been confused. Bernard Tanguy has mapped twenty-three places where the names *Divy* or *Davi* occur. But there is more confusion of names: between *Avi* and *Davi*, as both occur too. It is clear, however, that David/Dewi was a fairly popular saint in Brittany.

In the village of Saint-Divy there is no doubt. The parish church is not as attractive as Dirinon's, but it contains a remarkable feature. The chancel's timber ceiling has six large panels. Each is filled with a scene, painted in the late seventeenth century, from Rhygyfarch's *Life of St David*, with Latin explanations in the borders. So we see Sant's vision of the stag, the fish and the bees; Patrick giving way to the angel's prophecy and leaving for Ireland; Sant's meeting with Non and the birth of David; the baptism and education of David; David at the Synod of Brefi; David's death with heaven opening to receive him. All is colourful, done in a half-sophiscated, half-primitive style; some figures are elegant, some comical, especially a tubby David sitting on the hillock at Llanddewibrefi.

Perhaps more remarkable than either the Non and David churches or the chancel painting is the manuscript discovered in 1833 in the priest's house at Dirinon, now in the Bibliothèque nationale de France.

This is a Breton verse-drama of about 2,000 lines called *Buez Santez Nonn* [The Life of Saint Non]. This late medieval play must have been acted out every year in Dirinon, complete with a symbolic rape of Non on stage. It resembles other dramatisations of saints' lives in Breton and Cornish. There are Welsh religious plays from the same period, but none dealing with saints.

Buez Santez Nonn contains scenes about Non and David not found elsewhere. There are representations of Patrick's journey to the Isle of Rosina (!) in Ireland, and Non, said to be Irish herself, taking a vow of chastity before an abbess and her nuns. Sant is replaced, interestingly enough, by Queretic (Welsh Ceredig) who speaks courteously enough with Non before suddenly ravishing her and then immediately becoming penitent. Non laments her lost virginity, and realises that she is now pregnant. Merlin Emrys appears to prophesy the greatness of her son in Brittany. Then we have scenes with Gildas, whose sermons are intolerably long-winded, and with various tyrants. Halfway through the drama David is baptised and then educated by Paulinus. But then Non is taken ill: death gives her 'a blow to the heart' and she is taken to heaven by angels. David is ordained priest and performs miracles before his death and his own translation to paradise.

*

So much, inadequately, for David in Brittany: what about Ireland? We have seen that the Irish took an early interest in him as bishop and saint, but it is never asserted that he visited Ireland. However, his assocation with many Irish saints certainly gave him presence in the religious culture of Ireland, and he is named in a number of Irish saints' *Lives*. The arrival from Dyfed of the Cambro-Norman invaders in 1169–72 certainly must have given the saint's cult a considerable boost: it's possible that the churches dedicated to David in Ireland date from that period and after. Leinster and Dublin came principally under the influence of the invaders, and they are the districts where churches were dedicated – or rededicated – in David's name.

That 1169 invasion by an army, all from Dyfed, had attacked Ireland on the pretext of restoring the exiled king Dermot MacMurrough to the throne of Leinster. Thus began the conquest of Ireland. According to a near-contemporary poet, the war cry of these warriors was 'Dieu et Saint David'. It seems that the Norman lords of south-west Wales already saw themselves as a kind of 'Welsh-Normans', and Saint David as their patron saint and inspiration in war.

Unfortunately, it's difficult to determine how many David dedications exist in Ireland. Part of the problem, apparently, was a result of the disestablishment of the Irish Anglican Church in 1869. Many Anglican churches closed, while others may perhaps be nowadays in Catholic use. One respectable academic source names twelve medieval dedications in the name of David, but it is difficult to check them without a lengthy visit to Ireland. But one can certainly name the parishes of Siddan, Ardnurcher, Kilsallaghan and Naas as having medieval David churches. The register of David churches held by the see of St Davids names nine David churches in Ireland, but it includes some modern Catholic dedications, and is consequently not helpful. There is a modern Catholic church in the village of Oylegate, which may have been named for the well of St David nearby. The list of historic churches in Appendix I only contains those which I have been able to verify.

David's feast day on 1 March is important to every David church, and the traditions connected with his church in Naas are striking. On 3 March 1577, the chieftain Rory O'More launched an attack against Naas and to his surprise found the gates wide open and nobody on guard. Rory gathered that the townsfolk had indulged themselves so heavily on 1 March in honour of their patron saint that they had no spirit left for a fight. It is said that until the end of the eighteenth century the people of Naas wore leeks on 1 March.

St David's well, Oylegate, Wexford.

Photograph: Robert Davies

9

Saint David
and the Reformation

The first decades of the sixteenth century were a lively and fruitful period for Catholic Christianity in Wales. Two examples of many among the new church structural work of the period are the astonishing nave roof at St Davids cathedral, and the building of the Trinity chapel there. In those years new and rich ornaments were installed in churches across Wales, such as the great Jesse window in Llanrhaeadr-yng-Nghinmeirch in 1533. Pilgrims rode, walked or sailed to numerous sanctuaries the length and breadth of the country.

But a threat was in the air. Many different factors can explain the Reformation – too many to detail here. But to summarise: there was a growing resentment in parts of Europe of the corrupt power of the papacy, symbolised by the sale of indulgences – remissions of time in purgatory – to raise money. The most zealous Reformers attacked superstitions, argued for the translation of the Bible into vernacular languages, and were anxious to strip the Church of images.

In England and Wales Henry VIII had two problems.

First, he was up to his eyebrows in debt. Second, he wanted the pope to annul his first marriage so that he could remarry and beget a son and heir. He expected his able minister Thomas Cromwell to solve both problems. Cromwell's remedies were revolutionary. First, he showed Henry how to end the relationship between England and Wales and Rome by declaring, through Parliament, that he was head of the Church, not the pope. Thus he would be able to remarry. Second, he closed the monasteries, priories, nunneries and the friaries and confiscated their wealth.

Nor was that all. Cromwell had deep sympathy with the Reformation. He set to work to establish the legitimacy of the Bible in English translation. He ordered the abolition of saints' shrines and the confiscation of their relics and their wealth. He appointed sympathisers as bishops to help bring about these changes. Nemesis arrived in the diocese of St Davids with the appointment, in 1537, of William Barlow, a leading iconoclast, as bishop.

Barlow's spirit burned with desire to reform entirely the Church in west Wales. He loathed what he called the serving of ungodly images, vile idol-worship and papist pilgrimages. He intended to relocate the see to Carmarthen. He succeeded in moving the bishop's palace from St Davids to Abergwili, expelling the college of priests. But he utterly failed to move the bishop's throne to Carmarthen, leaving a day's journey or more between palace and cathedral. Virtually at a stroke, the cathedral lost its treasures, St Davids its bishop's palace, and its income from pilgrims dried up completely.

Barlow quarrelled fiercely with the stubbornly conservative clergy of St Davids. He seized relics, including two skulls encased in silver, and commandeered what he could of the church's books. Either then or later, the manuscripts which Rhygyfarch claimed to have consulted were destroyed, though not all at once: some were certainly concealed. Barlow stripped David's sanctuary of its valuables, sending the relics and precious ornaments to London. The valuable manor of Lamphey was gifted to the king, who was busy bleeding the wealth of the Church countrywide.

Barlow's name should not be blackened completely. By 1540 St Davids was inconveniently remote from the centre of its large diocese. St Davids remained a village, while Carmarthen was the largest town in Wales. Siting the cathedral there would have made diocesan administration much easier. But it would have been a catastrophe for the cathedral which, even stripped of so much, was still a splendid building – it could hardly have survived simply as a parish church. Today's tourist industry would not be half as valuable, and the cult of Saint David could never have been reconstituted in Carmarthen.

Under Barlow's successors, the martyred Protestant Robert Ferrar (bishop 1548–54, when he was burnt alive in Carmarthen), the Catholic Henry Morgan (1554–9) and the brief tenure of Thomas Young (1559–61), the diocese suffered like the rest of the country from the violent lurches of religious policy, until the initially fragile Elizabethan Church settlement began to function. St Davids was fortunate in acquiring Richard Davies as bishop in 1561. He was a Protestant of conviction who had taken refuge in Frankfurt during Mary's terror, and had learnt lessons both from his Continental period and the martyrdom of Ferrar. He realised that negative extremism would not function as an administrative policy. Rather, he saw the need to sustain Protestantism through the use of vernacular Bibles and Prayer Books, and did much towards this aim.

He had experience of translating the Bible into English, having helped with the production of the Bishops' Bible (1568), and worked with William Salesbury on a Welsh Prayer Book and New Testament (both 1567). His particular contribution was a foreword to the Prayer Book, 'A Letter to the Welsh People'. In it he outlined his understanding of the history of the early Church in Britain, showing how it could be linked to the new Reformed Protestant Church of England. In the beginning, he claims, Christianity in Britain was uncorrupted, except by the Pelagian heresy. And who, of course, had conquered that heresy but 'Archbishop David and other learned men of the kingdom'? But Vortigern had betrayed the cause by accepting the Saxons to Britain, and when Christianity came to them, it was the corrupted Roman version brought by Saint Augustine of Canterbury in 597. So the early Church in Britain had had healthy roots, and there was an honoured place for Saint David in the history of the Church – the Church of England, of course.

The Elizabethan Church settlement retained some 'Roman' features: bishops, simplified robes, altar crosses and a selection of saints. The native saints had been entirely omitted from the Prayer Book of 1549, but after 1558 the authorities were a little more tolerant. The Prayer Book of 1559 has a limited number of saints in its calendar: the Apostles and certain other figures of the New Testament, the early martyrs – and Saint David, on his festal day.

Yet, although David survived into the new regime, it must be acknowledged that the presence of the saints didn't count for much. Morning prayer and evening prayer – matins and vespers – replaced the monastic hours, and Holy Communion was less often celebrated than mass had been. The saints suffered another eclipse during the Commonwealth period (1649–60) when the Church of England virtually ceased to exist. When the Church was officially restored after the return of Charles II in 1660, Protestants complained that the saints had again survived in the Prayer Book calendar of 1662. The authorities rejected the protest, claiming that they had been restored simply in order to maintain their memory and for the secular purpose of dating legal documents.

We shall see that David attracted plenty of attention from the sixteenth century onwards, but that was given to him as a secular figure, with the emphasis on him as patron of Wales rather than simply a man of exemplary virtue. It is true that from 1715 there was a prestigious annual church service on each St David's Day, but it was only from the 1840s that the saints returned to eminence in the Church of England, thanks to the Oxford Movement. This is not the place to discuss the history of Anglo-Catholicism in Wales, but the movement brought benefits to the figure of David. The first was the effort to found, restore and improve church buildings, especially the cathedral at St Davids, which was in severe danger of collapse. Attention was eventually given to a bundle of bones, considered to be relics, but which received little attention until the early decades of the twentieth century. In 1925 they were placed in the Trinity Chapel, in a special chest, the gift of the Eastern Orthodox Church. When David's shrine was recently restored, the bones were placed in it and the chest left in place. Forensic examination had shown that the bones were of the twelfth century or later.

Another benefit was the attention paid to David in the first Church in Wales hymnbook, *Emynau'r Eglwys* (1941, 1951). This was produced by a High Church group within the Church in Wales, and caused much debate. The volume contained hymns for the seasons and festivals of the Church year, with a particular emphasis on the saints of Wales, and no fewer than five hymns honouring David. The first imprint had a remarkable appendix of Welsh religious poetry from *The Black Book of Carmarthen* onwards. The moving spirit of the book was W H Harris (1884–1956), a priest with parish experience before his appointment as professor of Welsh at St David's College, Lampeter. Harris was a man of strong Anglo-Catholic beliefs, as was his clerical colleague Silas Harris, author of a valuable study, *St David in the Liturgy* (1940). He had contributed two of the five hymns to David. Nowadays *Emynau'r Eglwys* has lost favour; many churches use a choice of interdenominational hymnals. In one of the most popular, *Caneuon Ffydd* [Songs of Faith], only one hymn mentions David, although a number are marked as suitable for singing on 1 March.

It must be remembered, of course, that David, as a Christian hero, was and is entirely ignored by the Nonconformist denominations which were until recently so powerful in the religious life of Wales. The only saints acceptable, as such, to them are those of the New Testament. Charles Edwards, the first Welsh Protestant historian, acknowledged David's status in his remarkable *Hanes y Ffydd Ddi-ffuant* [The History of the Genuine Faith], 1677, but other early Welsh-language historians, Simon Thomas, Theophilus Evans and Joshua Thomas, have little or no place for the Welsh saints.

*

The complex nature of the figure of Saint David is fundamental to this small book. Even when the country was thoroughly Christianised, there were early signs of David the secular hero. This is clear from the tenth-century *Armes Prydein Fawr* and the Cambro-Welsh war cries in twelfth-century Ireland. The secular David is a patriotic hero and inspiration as an embodiment of Wales to all, whether believers or not, whether pacifists or not. The rest of this chapter is devoted to the secular David – a figure already recognisable to Bishop Barlow.

Barlow had written a letter full of fire and brimstone to Thomas Cromwell in 1539:

[Like the bishop of Rome] even thus hath our Welsh David been advanced to be patron of Wales, as he that had seignory not only in earth by lawless privileged exemption, but by power also in Heaven to give it to whom he would… whose Legend is so uncertain of truth and certainly full of lies, that not only his saintly holiness is to be suspected, but rather to be doubted whether any such person was ever bishop there… I have certain pamphlets… [also mentioning] such enormous falsehood that scarcely Rome might be comparable with Saint David's territory concerning presumptuous usurpation upon their princes, crafty encroaching of possessions, subtle defeating of inheritances, extortion, bribery, simony, heresy, idolatry, superstition etc.

'Patron of Wales' was the bitter judgement of the ferocious Reformer about David.

Barlow was right – by his time David had been the patron saint and protector of Wales ever since the tenth century. In 1485, when Henry Tudor landed in Wales, the Welsh greeted him with the cry: 'Let us goe on in God's name, and St David, and we shall prevail.' After his surprising victory at Bosworth and his crowning there, Henry, parsimonious though he may seem to us, was ready to spend money to acknowledge his debt to Saint David. When his chief supporter Rhys ap Thomas was made a Knight of the Garter, he celebrated by staging a grand tournament at his home, Carew Castle. Over it floated a banner showing Saint David and Saint George embracing each other. The poet Rhisiart ap Rhys commemorated the occasion in a poem naming Henry, Rhys and David together.

The stream of Welsh people who followed the new king to London meant that the city became a kind of Welsh capital-in-exile for people who had never had a capital centre, although Ludlow was a lesser version until the abolition of the Council of Wales and the Marches in 1689. Henry VII's accounts show that his court celebrated St David's Day every year, and his son Henry VIII gave a bonus each year to Welsh members of his personal guard. But after the death of Elizabeth I in 1603, the link between the royal court and Welsh Londoners withered.

English literature of the period has plenty of evidence for interest in David. Shakespeare's *Henry V* presents Fluellen as a comic but not ridiculous character: 'there is much valour in this Welshman.' Henry himself boasts that he is a Welshman, the wearing of leeks is firmly associated with St David's Day, and the English braggart Pistol is forced to eat one.

The work of Shakespeare's contemporary Ben Jonson, the masque *For the Honour of Wales* (1618), is more ambiguous. By the time it was written a comic element is dominant. The praise of Wales is mingled with dancing goats and Welshmen mangling the English language. Jonson took much of his information from Camden's *Britannia*, including a reference to Bangu, Saint David's bell. But with the passing of time, the Saint David of English literary tradition becomes largely a folk-figure, with the remarkable exception of *The Most Famous History of the Seaven Champions of Christendome* described in the next chapter. It's clear from ballads in particular that the English were always ready to look down their noses at the Welsh and to make fun of them.

According to the scanty seventeenth-century evidence gathered by R T Jenkins and Helen Ramage, St David's Day could occasionally be a day of riot and violence. In 1640, a Welshman was brought to court for the manslaughter of a mocking Englishman. They quote a typically ambiguous song from 1642:

> This is a good week, when we wear a Leek,
> And carouse in Bacchus's fountains –
> We had better be here than in poor small beer,
> Or in our country mountains.

Samuel Pepys noted for 1 March 1667 that someone had hung out of his window a mocking dummy of a Welshman. In 1670, the hope of Lady Wynn of Gwydir, writing to her husband Sir John at the time of St David's Day, was that none of the 'enemies of Taffy' would lose an ear because of a lack of respect.

There is something strange about the history of Wales from 1603 to 1714. It was a century of much excitement and many major events. But where the Welsh had previously been able to see themselves as some kind of lesser partners in the kingdom of the Tudors, the arrival of a Scottish family on the throne changed the relationship quite drastically. The Welsh could continue to claim that the Stuarts were descended from Henry VII. Michael Drayton, in his huge poem *Poly-Olbion* (1612), could still praise the landscape of Wales and her patron saint:

As he did only drink what crystal Hodney yields,
And fed upon the Leeks he gather'd in the fields.
In memory of whom, in the revolving year,
The Welsh-men on his day that sacred herb do wear.

English ballads refer to the Welsh from time to time, and occasionally one goes further. *The Welchman's Glory* (pre-1689) celebrates the sacred herb and the festal day:

The Honour, Glory and the Grace
  Of valiant Brutes tryumphant Race,   [Brutus's]
Shewing the Reasons, wherefore they
  Wear Leeks upon St. Davids Day.
The valiant Deeds of Britans bold,   [Britons]
  I here shall sing in Verse;
Direct my Pen, Heroick Muse!
  While I the same reherse:
That to the Britans noble Fame,
  I bravely chant it may,
The Reason why, they do wear LEEKS
Upon St. Davids Day.

Brutus of course was the legendary ancestor of the Welsh, and still believed in at the time by many Welsh people. The balladeer explains that the Welsh had gained a great victory over the English on St David's Day. Another ballad, *The Praise of St David's Day*, repeats the message:

Who list to reade the deeds
  by valiant Welch-men done,

Shall find them worthy men of Armes,
　as breathes beneath the sunne:
They are of valiant hearts,
　of nature kind and meeke,
An honour on Saint David's day,
　it is to weare a Leeke.

The most striking image on any Welsh broadside is that of 1781 under the title 'Saint David for Wales'.

'Saint David for Wales', chapbook title-page, 1781.

It used all the clichés which demonstrate Welshness: goats, leeks, mountains, the harp, not to mention 'Welch Ale' and toasted cheese. Below is this verse:

> The Glorious Ancient British Saint Behold,
> David the Great in Fames Records Inroll'd.
> Loaded with Grand Repast his Sons to Treat
> And sets before them fine Welch Ale & Meat
> Herrings, Leeks, Black Puddings, Mustard, toasted Cheese
> With Goats Milk, Butter & such food as these
> Then brings his Minstrells Harp of graceful sound
> Whose Musick cheers their Hearts and makes their Voice
>   Resound.

Although without literary merit, these ballads are more entertaining than the sneering anti-Welshness of some popular eighteenth-century satires. But much stranger things had already happened to the figure of Saint David in English literature.

10

Saint David
in a World of Fantasy

Are you willing to believe in Saint David, the knight
in armour and, still more fantastic, Saint David the
married man? That is surely near to blasphemy – what
would Rhygyfarch have said! We have seen that David
was invoked as leader of the Britons in *Armes Prydein
Fawr* – but as an inspiration, not as a warrior. Anyway,
who in 1600 knew about *Armes Prydein Fawr*? The
sole copy of that manuscript had disappeared into the
Hengwrt Library in deepest Merionethshire, and didn't
emerge until the nineteenth century. But in 1596–7
there appeared the two parts of an exceptionally bizarre
work, *The Most Famous History of the Seaven Champions
of Christendome* by Richard Johnson, a prolific hack-
writer of the period. There was a one-volume edition in
1608 and a further edition with seven added chapters
in 1616. Another edition appeared in 1686 with an
added Third Part, probably by another hand. Reprints
and chapbook digests continued to appear sporadically
for the next two centuries with varying titles.

The seven champions are the seven patron
saints: George (England), Patrick (Ireland), Andrew

(Scotland), Denis (France), James (Spain), Anthony (Italy) and David (Wales). Yet this is no religious volume of devotion, nor a work of hagiography, but a kind of rambling and long-winded soap-opera romance, in which the seven champions go separately around the known world looking for adventures. They are saints only in name, being dressed in armour, killing pagans and monsters, saving damsels in distress and sometimes marrying them.

Since Johnson was an Englishman, George is, of course, the leader of this unsaintlike band. David gets plenty of space, and after a number of foreign adventures he returns to Wales. His symbol is a golden cross, an interesting anticipation of the golden cross on the modern flag of Saint David. He finds the land is being ravaged by pagans, so he calls on the surviving Welsh to join him and slaughter the disgusting enemy. He had to inspire them first, saying:

> To arms! I say, brave followers; I will be the first to give death the onset; and for my colours or ensign do I wear upon my burgonet, you see, a green leek beset with gold, which shall, if we win the victory, hereafter be an honour unto Wales; and on this day, being the first of March, be it for ever worn by the Welshmen in remembrance hereof.

The Welsh are victorious, but David dies of his wounds.

That's not the end, however. The other six champions also die in their turn, and in the second edition their sons go out on similar adventures. David's son is Sir Owen of the Mountains, 'son of the renowned champion St David of Wales, begotten on the body of the beautiful Estrild, daughter of the king of Powisland'.

Why mention all this nonsense? Because the story of the seven champions was extremely popular, and kept alive the name of David and the symbolism of the leek. It surely contributed to the references in the ballads quoted in the previous chapter, and to Nathaniel Griffith's remarkable poem *The Leek*, the subject of the rest of this chapter and the start of the next.

*

The Leek was published in 1717, with a second edition the following year emblazoned with the royal coat of arms. It is, perhaps, the most extraordinary poem in English ever published by a Welsh writer, apparently patriotic, but loaded with political significance. Nathaniel Griffith was a minor squire, a member of the Griffith family of Rhual, Flintshire. He is otherwise remembered as the man who raised a memorial to Germanus's Alleluia Victory on the supposed battleground north of Mold.

Griffith's poem, published as a large pamphlet, was dedicated to the Honourable and Loyal Society of Antient Britons and published in honour of Caroline of Ansbach, princess of Wales. It is 826 lines in length, in the decasyllabic rhyming couplets so popular at the time. The poem tells, in mock-heroic style, of the war between the Welsh and the Anglo-Saxons (never described as English). At first the Welsh are in despair:

they have been driven back by the ancient enemy, and are still losing ground and their leaders.

At last a new leader appears:

> Then David rose, a venerable Seer,
> In Sanctity of Life without a Peer,
> By Heaven ordain'd fresh Ardor to infuse;
> And in these Words their Courage he renews.
> And is it thus, our Country we defend?
> Must then the *British* Name inglorious end?
> Not so our Fathers shun'd the fatal Field,
> Or to the Conqu'rors of the World did yield:
> Not so these very Saxons e'er cou'd boast
> The smallest Share of our dear Country lost.
> Is it for Love of Life, we've Cowards grown?
> O, what is Life, when *Liberty* is gone?

Before preparing his arms, so to speak, David spends a week of prayer at St Davids:

> O Power Supreme! Whose everlasting Sway
> Nature and all her varying Turns obey…
> Gracious, thy *Britain* now behold! e'er while
> Thy chosen Nation, and thy favour'd *Isle*!…

David admits the many sins of the Britons and the weakness which drove them to invite the Saxons into their land in the first place. These confessions fire enthusiasm in his breast, and tribes from all over Wales come to Caerleon to join his host. When David steps forward to address his troops, the soil rises under his feet (echoes of the Synod of Brefi!) so that all can hear his powerful summary of early British history. When he is challenged to fight by a braggart Saxon chief, David is ready:

> Then with full Force, he the pois'd Jav'lin threw,
> And certain of the Mark it whizzing flew:
> Full in his gaping Mouth the Weapon sped,
> And nail'd his venom'd Tongue up to his Head…

Rhygyfarch would have hardly endorsed this violent behaviour. The Saxons are thoroughly defeated:

> Whole Ranks mow'd down together load the Plain,
> And on, the *Britons* climb o'er Hills of Slain…

Unexpectedly, it was the Saxons who were wearing leeks in battle, but David's men seize them from the corpses as trophies. Night comes, and the weary warriors sleep. But the glory of the day will live on, for it is 1 March:

> This Day, that still its David's Name shall bear,
> And LEEKS adorn in each revolving Year!

Griffith was surely familiar with the story of the seven champions, but the differences are interesting. His vision of how the Welsh acquired the leek as their symbol is odd, but the poem is great fun, and far more entertaining than the leaden prose of Richard Johnson. However, there is far more to the poem than meets the eye.

THE
LEEK.
A
POEM
ON
St DAVID's DAY.

Moſt Humbly Inſcrib'd to the Honourable

SOCIETY of *ANTIENT BRITONS*,
Eſtabliſh'd in Honour of Her ROYAL HIGHNESS's
Birth-Day, and the Principality of WALES.

By *N. GRIFFITH*, Eſq;

Pan fo ſôn am Ddigoniant,
Dy roi'n vwch pob Dewr a wnant !   *Tudur Penllyn.*

LONDON:
Printed by W. WILKINS, for W. HINCHLIFFE, at *Dryden's*
Head under the *Royal-Exchange.* MDCCXVII.

The Leek, Nathaniel Griffith, title-page, 1st edition.

11

The Secular Saint David and his Festal Day

When David slept after the victory described in *The Leek*, he had a dream which showed him the future of the Welsh and the English; they are all eventually to be blessed with the arrival of a new king from Germany. In his train will come liberty, trade and brotherhood, and there will be a new princess of Wales, Caroline of Ansbach, whose birthday by good fortune was on 1 March.

To grasp the situation fully, we need to understand what was happening in 1714–15. Queen Anne, who had died in 1714, was the last of the Stuart sovereigns. She died without a living child despite fifteen pregnancies, but there were heirs, principal of whom was James Stuart her half-brother, son of James II who had lost the throne in the revolution of 1688. However, all living descendants of James II were barred from the throne for being Roman Catholics, so the succession devolved on George, Elector of Hanover, as George I.

This settlement was strongly favoured by some politicians ('Whigs'), while others ('Tories') were less sympathetic, and a considerable number of people favoured James Stuart, 'the Old Pretender', who mounted an invasion of Scotland in 1715 in the hope of raising the country against the Hanoverians and regaining his father's throne. The majority of Welsh Members of Parliament – all gentry of course – favoured the Tories, but there were a small minority of Whigs in the country. Nathaniel Griffith was one of the Welsh Whigs strongly supporting the Hanoverians.

As it happened, George I's son, another George, was the first prince of Wales since 1649. This had resulted from the failure of Charles II, James II and the queens regnant Mary and Anne to have a son able to assume that title. But Welsh Hanoverian supporters seized on the double coincidence of the arrival of a prince of Wales, married to an attractive and intelligent princess born on St David's Day. In 1737, Richard Morris, a later founder of the Cymmrodorion Society, would write a sympathetic elegy in Welsh on Caroline's death.

All this is history and is reflected in the subtext of *The Leek*. The leaders of David's troops are given transparent aliases: Tredegar, Oudoen, Vauganus and Merig. These scarcely conceal John Morgan of Tredegar, Arthur Owen of Orielton, John Vaughan, Viscount Lisburne of Ceredigion, and Owen Meyrick of Bodorgan, Anglesey – all leading Whig Hanoverians in Wales.

Moreover, *The Leek* was dedicated to the Honourable and Loyal Society of Antient Britons. That Society was founded by Thomas Jones, a London-Welsh lawyer of whom not much seems to be known except for this episode in his life. In the early spring of 1715, he placed a notice in the *London Gazette*, advertising that the

Reverend George Lewis would preach 'in the Antient British tongue' at St Paul's church, Covent Garden, on 1 March. This would be followed by a dinner in the Haberdashers' Hall.

This may possibly have been the first Welsh sermon preached in London on St David's Day. But we know that in Dublin, which was a kind of capital for north-west Wales, the year 1704 had seen the publication of *A Discourse in praise of St. David, the saint and patron of the Welsh*. Thomas Jones's plan was more ambitious. The London sermon was duly delivered, followed by a march to the Haberdashers' Hall. There the Society of Antient Britons was constituted and officers elected from among both Welsh and English men present. It was decided to invite the new prince of Wales to become its president, and the sermon and dinner on St David's Day became an annual institution.

By 1716 the Antient Britons had presented a Loyal Address to the king, whose son had accepted the office of president. Thomas Jones was knighted, and published a remarkable booklet in 1717:

The Rise and Progress of the Most Honourable and Loyal Society of Antient Britons, established In Honour to Her Royal Highness's Birth-Day, and the Principality of Wales, on St. David's Day, the First of March, 1714–15. By Sir Thomas Jones, Kt, Treasurer and Secretary to the said Society. In a Letter to his Countrymen of the Principality of Wales. London, W.Wilkins, for W. Taylor, 1717.

It's a powerful plea for loyalty to the new king, and for

the Welsh to become more respectable and ambitious. It also notes the decision to raise money for the benefit of poor Welsh people. In 1715 the Society had raised money to support two Welsh boys as apprentices in London. In 1718 the Welsh School was established, which continued in several locations in London, and then in Kent, until it finally closed in 2009.

The establishment of the Society was a major step forward not only for the Welsh in London, but also in giving status to Wales as a whole. At last Wales had a form of representation, of recognition, however small. This was the first Welsh society of any kind. When the more ambitious Society of Cymmrodorion was established in 1751, it shared many officers and members with the Antient Britons. This was the first of the three Cymmrodorion societies, the third of which flourishes today. The Antient Britons, with their less ambitious programme of annual sermon, annual dinner and support for charities, lasted for more than two centuries.

A number of the St David's Day London sermons were printed: we know of sermons for 1716, 1717, 1723, 1728, 1731 and 1754 (this one was delivered in Bristol), and there were surely others, whether they were eventually printed or not. Richard Morris described the 1728 occasion in London:

> St. David's Day was observ'd here with great ceremony, the sermon was preach'd in English by Mr. John Morgan and the prayers in British by Mr. Phillips, at St. Clement's Danes...
> The 12 stewards and the Society walk'd in procession to

Merchant Taylor's Hall where they din'd, consisting of about a thousand people, Welsh and English, and made a handsome collection for the Charity Children descended from British parents which they keep.

The Times noted a number of meetings of the Antient Britons for dinner and charitable fundraising in the nineteenth and twentieth centuries. After a series of St David's Day meetings from 1922 till 1929, it seems that the Society faded. Nevertheless, a dinner was held in 1957 to celebrate the Welsh School's move to Ashford, Kent, a century earlier. In 1964 the Society advertised for a treasurer for the school. But, by 2009, it had all ended. A final ceremony was held on St David's Day 2015, with a Welsh sermon at St Paul's church, Covent Garden, where it had all begun three centuries earlier.

*

London and Dublin weren't the only cities to celebrate Saint David. In 1729, a number of Welsh migrants to the USA met in Philadelphia, Pennsylvania, to establish The Welsh Society of Philadelphia, now the oldest functioning Welsh society in the world. As in London, the initial intention was charitable, to provide for poor Welsh people in the city. A substantial number of Welsh Nonconformists (Quakers, Baptists and Independents) had moved to Pennsylvania during the seventeenth century. But the Society also celebrated St David's Day from its foundation, and still does so.

Back in London, as we have seen, the Honourable

Society of Cymmrodorion had been formed in 1751, with a coat of arms supported by a druid and by Saint David. The Cymmrodorion Society was ambitious, holding regular meetings, not in churches or guildhalls but in taverns; one of their intentions was to publish classics of Welsh literature. However, even the cultivated Richard Morris was as willing as other members to get hopelessly drunk on St David's Day, and doubtless at other meetings too.

There is no better expression of Welsh devotion to St David's Day than a poem by David Samwell, who later became the secretary of the Gwyneddigion Society in 1788. In 1776, he went as ship's doctor on the last expedition of Captain James Cook to the Pacific, and on 1 March he composed verses in Welsh for the occasion, including this (roughly translated) sentiment:

> In song and joy with hearts uniting
> We celebrate David's feast with delight long-lasting,
> Sitting in a snug, with no thought of leaving,
> All night – and Samuel never moving.

He calls to mind his fellow Gwyneddigion, noting that they will be celebrating on the same day, but not at the same hour, since he is on the other side of the world.

At some time during the seventeenth century, if not earlier, St David's Day received official recognition. It's one thing to see it mentioned on the back of Thomas Jones's almanacs at the turn of that century; rather more important is the fact that it's listed in *The Court and City Register* of London. The 1762 volume includes a list of all public holidays, at a time of course when these were the only breaks that workers could hope for. Some of these holidays are to do with royalty (the execution of Charles I, the birthday of George III, and so on). Others are for remembrance of secular occasions: the Fire of London, the Gunpowder Plot. The rest are religious days, naming Easter, All Saints, some of the Apostles – and there among them is St David's Day. David is the only national saint on the list – no George, Patrick or Andrew. At the same time it is clear that 1 March is a secondary holiday, like the Fire of London or the birthday of the Duke of Cumberland, and not observed in government offices or banks.

In Wales before 1800, St David's Day celebrations are difficult to trace, though they must certainly have happened. Welsh towns were small and there were no Welsh or local newspapers until the new century. The first newspaper in Wales was Swansea's *Cambrian*. In it there are notices of a dinner held for St David's Day by the Royal Glamorgan Militia in 1806, and a St David's Ball held in Llandeilo in 1810. There were celebrations in Aberystwyth in 1812; there were various dinners at Swansea hotels in 1820, and in 1823 there were celebrations held by the Swansea Cymmrodorion Society. All of this suggests that there must have been such occasions in the eighteenth century which were not recorded. Some later meetings were used to debate the disestablishment of the Church of England in Wales, and some Nonconformists remained suspicious of David's Catholic origins.

Churchmen were certainly willing to celebrate Saint David. In 1819, the Reverend John Taylor of Llanarthne published an English sermon entitled 'Cambrian Excellence', which was delivered at St Peter's, Carmarthen, on 1 March. Taylor spared no effort in gilding the lily: Wales is fortunate because Saint Paul preached here (!), because Brennus ('commonly called Brân the Blessed') had become a Christian, along with his son Caractacus [*sic*] when imprisoned in Rome. Brennus returned to Britain and converted the natives from Druidism to Christianity.

Eventually David emerges, and Taylor gives a rough account of the Rhygyfarch story. He far excels Rhygyfarch in his desire to praise David: 'Almost every mountain in the Menevian province witnessed the labours of the primate. From one extremity to the other did he announce good tidings, publishing peace, and declaring unto Zion that Jehovah reigneth.' All this, we are assured, is 'authentic history, freed from legendary tales'. Most of the sermon is devoted to praise of the post-Catholic bishops of St Davids, especially the martyred Robert Ferrar.

*

It is apparent, if not easily proven, that St David's Day celebrations grew in popularity during the nineteenth century, surely in connection with the national revival of patriotism from 1860 onwards. St David's Day dinners were frequent, and local versifiers enjoyed the chance to proclaim the saint's praises and see their work in the local press. But much more research is needed to show what kind of ebbs and flows of celebrations there were between 1800 and the present day. Historian Mike Benbough-Jackson has given a good lead in this field. His essay on celebrating St David's Day in St Davids diocese covers more ground than the title suggests (see the Bibliography under his name). Welsh regimental celebrations of the festival are described in my *Looking for Wales* (Tal-y-bont, 2013, pp.19–22).

By the nineteenth century celebrations of St David's Day followed the flag across the British Empire, and renewed migration to the USA brought more celebrations there too. Today one can trace Welsh societies across the English-speaking world (ironic phrase!), from Lackawanna County (Pennsylvania), to Brisbane, from Utica (New York State) to Singapore, Taiwan and Hong Kong. Add to them the many Cymmrodorion and Cambrian societies and Welsh (usually male) choirs, and celebration of St David's Day is still a worldwide phenomenon in the early twenty-first century.

Another aspect of the presence of David in modern life is the number of institutions of many kinds named for him, other than the patriotic societies. Awareness of the saint's importance meant that the Church college opened at Lampeter in 1827 was St David's College, now part of the University of Wales Trinity St David. There are, or have been, a number of St David's hospitals, including one in Carmarthen. Carmarthen also has a St David's Park. The Cardiff workhouse, opened in 1839, became St David's hospital by 1948 but is now closed.

All kinds of establishments and companies use Saint

David's name. One of the oldest is the St David's Club in Aberystwyth, which claims to have been founded in 1770 as a gentlemen's club. The St David's Society in Trelew, Patagonia, has been active since 1892. To take other examples at random, Cardiff has a private Catholic sixth form college, a major hotel, a shopping centre and concert hall all named for David. There is a St David's Square in London's Tower Hamlets, a St David's health centre in Minneapolis, a business centre in Newtown, Powys. The Freemasons have a St David's hall in Berwick-upon-Tweed, and in Tarbolton in Ayrshire where Robert Burns was a member! One could follow the trail around the world.

*

The following paragraph is by Dr Bruce Griffiths, who owns a copy of the work described. I did not previously know of its existence.

Thomas Dibdin's *St. David's Day: or, The Honest Welchman (&c)* (London, 1801) is a romantic ballad farce, set in a Welsh seaside village on St David's Day. A shipwrecked English lad, son of a wealthy Londoner, wins the heart of a Welsh lass whose father, the 'honest Welchman', succoured him. Some slight amusement is caused by the Welsh accents of the players and an inquiry into Welsh superstition, but the Welsh are warmly depicted as hospitable, honest and patriotic: the capture of French invaders by brave Welshwomen near Fishguard in 1797 is highly praised. St David's Day is celebrated with song, dance and harpists. Dibdin had visited Carmarthen and Haverfordwest and dedicated the play to their inhabitants, and to all the Welsh, for their hospitality.

St. DAVID's DAY:

OR, THE

HONEST WELCHMAN.

A BALLAD FARCE,

IN TWO ACTS.

AS PERFORMED AT THE

THEATRE-ROYAL, COVENT-GARDEN.

By THOMAS DIBDIN;

AUTHOR OF "THE JEW AND DOCTOR," "SCHOOL FOR PREJU-
DICE," "IL BONDOCANI," "FIVE THOUSAND A YEAR,"
"MOUTH OF THE NILE," "NAVAL PILLAR," "AL-
TERATIONS AND ADDITIONS IN THE BIRTH-
DAY," "HORSE AND WIDOW," &c. &c.

Title page of *St. David's Day: or, The Honest Welchman.*

My thanks to Ann Corkett and to Gareth Davies (photographer)

*

The study of Saint David was part of the awakening of medieval scholarship throughout Europe in the nineteenth century. The languages and history of the Celtic countries were studied, although the task of cleansing them of Ossianism and Iolo Morganwg's bardism took some time. The first lecturer in Welsh was Rice Rees, appointed at Lampeter in 1827. His remarkable work, *An Essay on the Welsh Saints* (1836) has a pioneering discussion of David, and is still worth reading today. W J Rees produced *Lives of the Cambro-British Saints* in 1853, containing the Latin text of Rhygyfarch's *Life* with English translation, as well as the Welsh-language *Buched Dewi*. The Latin reworking of Gerald of Wales's *Life of St David* was printed (for the only time so far) in 1863 as part of a compilation of all his writings; it was the subject of an unpublished MA thesis (Cardiff, 1934) by Trevor Bowen Jones.

The first monograph on David's life was published by the Irish scholar John O'Hanlon, *The Life of St David, Archbishop of Menevia, chief patron of Wales, and titular patron of Naas church and parish, in Ireland* (Dublin, 1869). O'Hanlon was a major scholar of the lives of Irish saints, and, as one would expect, he was thoroughly familiar with medieval sources. Unfortunately, despite all the author's hopes, and despite the book's many virtues, it doesn't appear to have been a success. In 1869 Welsh prejudices against both Catholicism and Ireland were fierce, and unsurprisingly there is only one copy in Wales, in the university library at Bangor.

The first edition of Rhygyfarch's *Life* was published with an English translation in *Y Cymmrodor* in 1910 by the Anglican priest-scholar A W Wade-Evans. Extra copies of the study were printed and bound in a volume entitled *St. David, Archbishop, Patron of Wales* (Stow-on-the-Wold, 1914). In 1923 Wade-Evans published his English translation of Rhygyfarch's Latin with notes, entitled *The Life of St David* (SPCK, 1923). It's an interesting study, with a number of quotations from other saints' *Lives* which mention David. Wade-Evans republished his version of the Latin text of Rhygyfarch along with other Welsh saints' *Lives* in *Vitae Sanctorum Britanniae et Genealogiae* (1944, reprinted under an English title in 2004). In 1967 Canon J W James published *Rhigyfarch's Life of St. David*, preferring the shorter Latin text.

Meanwhile, the oldest text of the Welsh *Life* of David had appeared in *Anecdota Oxoniensia: Texts, Documents, and Extracts* (Oxford, 1895), containing all the texts in the *Book of the Anchorite of Llanddewibrefi*. It appeared under the editorship of John Morris-Jones and John Rhŷs, although the latter attributed almost all the work to the former. It took many years for an annoted edition of the Welsh *Life* to appear, but it was undertaken by D Simon Evans in the Welsh language in 1959 and in English in 1988.

While Wade-Evans, J W James and D Simon Evans worked on the texts, a new era of discussion was opened by the historical geographer Emrys Bowen in *The Settlements of the Celtic Saints in Wales* (1956) and his more sophisticated *Saints, Seaways and Settlements* (1960), and in a popular bilingual booklet *Saint David/ Dewi Sant* (1983). David Dumville made a valuable contribution in a published lecture in 2001, *Saint David of Wales*. In 2007 there appeared the volume to which this book is much indebted, *St David of Wales: Cult, Church and Nation* (edited by J Wyn Evans and Jonathan Wooding), including a new edition and translation of the longer version of Rhygyfarch's text, and authoritative chapters on a range of related subjects by various scholars.

*

Thus ends, apart from the Appendices and the Bibliography, this attempt at a pioneering study of the figure of Saint David of Wales through the centuries. In Greek legend the hero Proteus, a sea-god, could, like the sea, change his appearance so that he was never the same. David too is a protean figure in human imagination: a monk and abbot, priest and archbishop, teetotaller and vegetarian, miracle worker, prophet and war leader, both chaste and in fantasy a married man and father, in faith a Catholic – honoured as a Protestant.

Appendix I

The Churches
of Saint David

While Welsh people celebrate Saint David as a secular figure of patriotism in societies across the world, the foundation of his fame is as a saint of the Church. By the present day, hundreds of David churches have been founded in many countries. The purpose of this appendix is to list those churches which we know to have been established in the Middle Ages (before c.1500), followed by an outline of the worldwide situation. The subject is not necessarily easy, since every David isn't necessarily the Welsh David.

The medieval David churches are to be found in Wales, England, Ireland and Brittany. A few of these are unexpected. Thus there is a David church in Airmyn, Yorkshire – a great distance from any other. Nevertheless, there's no doubt that the David of Airmyn has been recognised for centuries as the David of Wales. The present church was built in 1676 to replace an earlier building founded in 1311. The circumstances of the original foundation are unknown. The present church contains in the ceiling beams a plaster figure of a dove, a bird always associated with David, and a window in memory of a local soldier killed in the Boer War shows saints George and David in company.

Other efforts have been made to list medieval David churches. The most valuable, though covering only the historic diocese of St Davids, is by Heather James in a chapter in *St David of Wales: Cult, Church and Nation*. Below is my imperfect effort to list all David churches founded before 1500. In Wales and England they are divided into the historic counties:

Pembrokeshire
St Davids cathedral, Brawdy, Whitechurch, St Dogwells, Hubberston, Prendergast, Llanllawern, Llanychlwydog, Llanychâr, Bridell, Maenordeifi

The interior of St David's church, Maenordeifi.

Ceredigion

Bangor Teifi, Henllan, Blaen-porth, Capel Dewi (Llandysul), Llanddewibrefi, Llannarth, Henfynyw, Llanddewi Aber-arth, Blaenpennal

Carmarthenshire

Llanddewi Felffre, Henllan Amgoed, Meidrim, Abergwili, Capel Dewi (Llwynhendy), Betws (Ammanford), Llanarthne, Capel Dewi (Llandeilo), Llanycrwys, Llangadog

Breconshire

Llywel, Trallong, Llan-faes, Llanddew, Garthbrengi, Llanddewi Abergwesyn, Llanwrtyd, Llanddewi Llwyn-y-fynwent, Llanynys, Llanddewi Maesmynys, Llanddewi'r Cwm

Radnorshire

Cregrina, Glascwm, Colfa, Rhiwlen, Llanddewi Fach, Llanddewi Ystrad Enni, Heyop, Whitton

Glamorgan

Llanddewi Fach (Gower), Llangyfelach, Laleston, Llanddewi

Monmouthshire

Llanover Fawr, Llanthewi Skirrid, Llantrisant Fawr, Llanthony, Trostre

Herefordshire
Kilpeck, Much Dewchurch, Little Dewchurch

Yorkshire
Airmyn

Devon
Exeter, Thelbridge, Ashprington

Somerset
Barton St David

Gloucestershire
Moreton-in-Marsh

Cornwall
Davidstow (David's name is associated with other places in Cornwall, such as Praa Sands and Perran Sands.)

Brittany
Dirinon, Saint-Divy (see chapter 8)

Ireland
Naas, Kilsallaghan, Siddan, Ardnercher (see chapter 8)

The most valuable list of all worldwide David churches, historic and modern, is held at St Davids cathedral.

Unfortunately, it isn't online. The list names 364 churches, so that one is prayed for every day of the year, with the odd day to pray for all other David churches, of which there are at least a few. The list is mostly of Anglican churches, but the Roman Catholics, Eastern Orthodox, the United Reformed Church, the Presbyterian Church of Wales, the Baptists, Methodists, and other denominations all appear. By nation or region they appear in the diocesan list as follows, with total numbers in brackets:

Wales (136), USA (84), Canada (47), England (36), Australia (21), New Zealand (11), the Caribbean Islands (10), Ireland (9), Southern Africa (6), Papua New Guinea (3), the Philippines (1).

Some dedications to David (not included in the above figures) are not to the Welsh saint: one or two churches in the USA honour King David of the Old Testament, while at least one church in Scotland honours King David I of Scotland (1124–53), known as David the Saint. There are three cathedrals honouring David: the Church in Wales cathedral at St Davids, the Roman Catholic cathedral in Cardiff, and the Anglican cathedral in Hobart, Tasmania. In Hobart the choice of St David was actually a gesture to honour Lieutenant-Colonel David Collins, the first governor of Van Diemen's Land (now Tasmania). Nevertheless, Saint David is recognised there.

Appendix II

A Digest of Rhygyfarch's *Life of St David*

Note: I have rendered the words *Brittones* and *Britannia* as 'Britons' and 'Britain', rather than as 'the Welsh' and 'Wales'. This is a hard decision: I would argue that Rhygyfarch understood correctly that 'Welsh' and 'Wales' were not viable concepts in the sixth century; he would have known that even in his own day they were still valid terms for the Welsh, Cornish and Cumbrians.

1–2 (the numbers refer to chapters in Rhygyfarch's book). God foretells the coming of certain people by signs and revelations. Thus an angel told Sant, king of Ceredigion, that he would find three gifts in the Teifi valley, a stag, a fish, and a honeycomb which foretell his future son's gifts of spiritual power and abstinence.

3. The virtuous Bishop Patrick came to Dyfed and chose to dwell in *Vallis Rosina*. But an angel told him that the land would be evangelised by someone to be born in thirty years' time. Patrick was disheartened, but was told by an angel to go to Ireland, and was shown that land. Patrick sailed from Porth Mawr after resurrecting a dead man from twelve years in his grave.

4–5. Sant came to Dyfed and saw the beautiful nun, Non, whom he raped. She became pregnant. When she entered a church where Saint Gildas was preaching, he fell silent, and was only able to resume when she left the building. Gildas foretold that her son would become the greatest of all the saints of Britain, and that he himself would leave for another place.

6–11. A local tyrant sought to kill Non's baby when he was born, but a great storm concealed her during her labour in a protected place. During her pains the rock she leant on broke in sympathy. A church now occupies the place. When Ailbe, bishop of Munster, came to baptise the baby a spring burst forth, and blind Mobi was healed by the baptismal water. David was educated in *Vetus Rubus*, living a chaste life of study, and was ordained priest. He then went elsewhere to Paulinus the teacher, once a pupil of Saint Germanus. He spent years studying the Bible, and healed Paulinus when he went blind.

12–17. David is commanded to profit from his education by going on a mission. He founded twelve monasteries, at Glastonbury (he cleansed the hot springs of Bath), Crowland (Lincolnshire), Repton (Derbyshire), Colfa and Glascwm (both in Powys), Leominster (Herefordshire), Raglan (Gwent) and Llangyfelach (Glamorgan) before returning to *Vetus Rubus*. In a vision he learned that he should move from there to somewhere more blest. So with three followers he moved to *Vallis Rosina*, called Hodnant by the Britons, and he lit a fire there. The smoke was seen by Baia, the local tyrant, who foresaw David's power, and plotted with his wife to kill him, but in vain. Then Baia asked David's forgiveness and granted him *Vallis Rosina* for ever. But Baia's wife sent girls to wanton naked in front of the monks. They appealed to David to drive the girls away, but he bade them be strong.

18–22. Baia's wife slew her virtuous step-daughter Dunod, and then disappeared. Baia sought revenge again, but fire fell on his house and he died. After God had destroyed David's enemies, the saint established his famous monastery. The discipline was harsh, based on hard work. The monks took the yoke on their shoulders to draw the plough without oxen. They worked with spades and shovels, hoe and saw, and provided all their needs. They despised wealth, working quietly and prayerfully.

23–32. After the day's work, they studied in silence until the bell called them to the church, where they sang Psalms. They lived in moderation, according to health and age. The sick and aged would be better fed. Having given thanks, they would go back to the church, before sleeping until cockcrow. David was their confessor, and they obeyed him in all things. They had no personal property: animal skins were their clothing. A novice had to come as if naked, and would gain admittance after ten days' waiting at the gate. David prayed all the time, taking counsel with the angels, and remaining free from temptations of the flesh. He himself would minister to orphans, widows, the sick, the needy and the pilgrims, in imitation of the monks of Egypt.

33–41. David performed a host of miracles. He prayed for a spring to give water to the monastery, and for wine for mass. He obtained another spring for a farmer whose land was dry. His follower Aidan saved the oxen and cart which had fallen into the sea, before he went to Ireland to establish a monastery there. When Aidan heard that two of David's servants were planning to poison him, he warned him by supernatural means. David gave some of the poisoned food to animals, which died, but he ate some himself without difficulty. He gave his own horse to the Irish visitor Bairre to return to Ireland: he rode it over the waves, meeting Saint Brendan on the back of a whale before reaching the island. David saved the life of his follower Modomnóc when he had been attacked.

42–43. A large part of Ireland served David the Waterman, thanks to Aidan. When the latter sailed to Ireland, he forgot the bell that David had given him. When David heard this, he told the bell to go to his master, and an angel bore it to Aidan. Modomnóc took a swarm of bees to Ireland, but then returned to see David, followed by the bees. He went again to Ireland, but the bees followed him. When he had returned to David in Wales three times, David told the bees to go back to Ireland, and never return. To this day bees will not remain in the monastery.

44–48. David went with Padarn and Teilo to Jerusalem. David was given the apostolic gift of tongues when they arrived in the city. An angel had told the patriarch to consecrate them bishops, and had prepared seats of great honour for them: and he elevated David to be an archbishop. 'Go out to preach to the Jews,' the patriarch told them, and they obeyed with success. Then he gave gifts to David: an altar, a miraculous bell and staff, and a gold cloak. The other saints were given gifts too, and the gifts were carried home by angels; David received his at Llangyfelach.

49–58. Because of a resurgence of the Pelagian heresy, even after the two visits of Saint Germanus, a Synod was called at Brefi of all the British bishops, with a host of churchmen, kings, princes, lay men and women. But nobody could hear the preaching, so a great pile of clothes was made for the speakers to stand on, but still many could not hear. David's former teacher Paulinus told them to invite David, who was, at first, too modest to accept, but was brought by Dyfrig and Deiniol to the place, having first resurrected a widow's dead son, Magna. A cloth was laid on the ground for David to stand on, and the ground rose under him so that all could hear him clearly, and a white dove settled on his shoulder. A church is on that hill now. The heresy was routed, so that all blessed David, and appointed him archbishop, and his monastery an archbishopric, whoever might govern it. The true decrees of the Church were written in his holy hand. There was rejoicing everywhere: David was made bishop, protector, preacher, teacher and almsgiver, and he shone with the glory of miracles. David was granted every possible authority and privilege of immunity with precedence over all as head and prince of all the Britons, until he had reached the age of 147.

59–65. On 22 February an angel told David that on 1 March Jesus and his angels would come for him. David was joyful, but the monks were terrified. He told them. 'Be steadfast. Bear to the end the yoke that you have unanimously accepted; and whatever you have seen and heard with me, keep it and fulfil it.' The news spread through Britain and Ireland, and crowds came from all sides. David preached to them on the next Sunday and celebrated mass. He said to them all: 'My brothers, persevere in those things that you have learned from me, and have seen with me; on Tuesday, 1 March, I shall enter the way of the fathers; farewell in the Lord, for I shall go away. We shall not see each other any more in this world.' The people all lamented, but David was taken up by Jesus. And while all mourned, the holy brethren buried his body in the monastery.

66–7. These few works of holy David have been collected out of the most ancient writings of our country, especially from his own monastery, although much damaged. I, Rhygyfarch, have done what I can so that the readers may pray for me, so that I may find a place in Heaven. Amen.

Bibliography

Ian Atherton, 'Commemorating Conflict and the Ancient British Past in Augustan Britain', *Journal for Eighteenth-Century Studies*, Vol. 36, No. 3 (2013), pp. 377–93.

S Baring-Gould & John Fisher, *Lives of the British Saints*, Vol. II, London, 1908.

Mike Benbough-Jackson, 'St David meets the Victorians', *Journal of Victorian Culture Online*, 22 February 2013.

Mike Benbough-Jackson, 'Celebrating a Saint on His Home Ground: St David's Day in St Davids Diocese during the Nineteenth Century', chapter 6 in *Religion and Society in the Diocese of St Davids 1485–2011*, eds W. Gibson & J. Morgan-Guy, Ashgate, 2015.

Steve Boardman & John Reuben Davies (eds), *Saints' Cults in the Celtic World*, Woodbridge, 2009.

Kathleen Bramley *et al.*, *Gwaith Llywelyn Fardd ac Eraill o Feirdd y Ddeuddegfed Ganrif*, Cardiff, 1994.

Martin Carver (ed.), *In Seach of Cult: Archaeological Investigations in Honour of Philip Rahtz*, Woodbridge, 1993.

T M Charles-Edwards, *Wales and the Britons 350–1064*, Oxford, 2013.

Bernadette Cunningham & Raymond Gillespie, 'The cult of St David in Ireland before 1700', in J R Guy and & W G Neely, *Contrasts and Comparisons: Studies in Irish and Welsh Church History*, Welshpool/Dublin, 1999, pp. 24–46.

Wendy Davies, *Patterns of Power in Early Wales*, Oxford, 1990.

David N Dumville, *St David of Wales*, Cambridge, 2001.

Owain Tudor Edwards, *Matins, Lauds and Vespers for St David's Day*, Cambridge, 1990.

D Simon Evans, *The Welsh Life of St David*, Cardiff, 1988.

J Wyn Evans & Jonathan M Wooding (eds), *St David of Wales: Cult, Church and Nation*, Woodbridge, 2007.

Martin Fitzpatrick, Nicholas Thomas & Jennifer Newell (eds), *The Death of Captain Cook and other Writings by David Samwell*, Cardiff, 2007.

Elissa Henken, *Traditions of the Welsh Saints*, Cambridge, 1987.

Elissa Henken, *The Welsh Saints: a Study in Patterned Lives*, Woodbridge, 1991.

J E de Hirsch-Davies, *Catholicism in Medieval Wales,* London, 1916.

J W James, *Rhigyfarch's Life of St. David*, Cardiff, 1967.

Francis Jones, *The Holy Wells of Wales*, Cardiff, 1992.

J B Midgley, *Dewi Sant: Saint David: Patron of Wales*, Leominster, 2012.

Daniel J Mullins, *Seintiau Cynnar Cymru*, Llanrwst, 2002.

John O'Hanlon, *The Life of St. David, Archbishop of Menevia, Chief Patron of Wales…*, Dublin, 1869.

Morfydd E Owen (ed.), *Gwaith Llywelyn Fardd I ac Eraill*, Cardiff, 1994.

Geraint Phillips, *Dyn Heb ei Gyffelyb yn y Byd: Owain Myfyr a'i Gysylltiadau Llenyddol*, Cardiff, 2010.

Sarah Prescott, *Eighteenth-century Writing from Wales: Bards and Britons*, Cardiff, 2008.

Bernard Tanguy, 'The Cults of St Nonne and Saint Divi in Brittany', in Evans and Wooding, *St David of Wales*, translated by Karen Jankulak from 'Les Cultes de Sainte Nonne et de Saint Divi en Bretagne', in Yves Le Berre *et al.*, *Buez Santez Nonn: mystère breton: vie de Sainte Nonne*, Brest, 1999.

John Taylor, *Cambrian Excellent. A Sermon, on St David's Day… on the 1st of March, 1819*, London, 1819.

Alan Thacker & Richard Sharpe (eds), *Local Saints and Local Churches in the Early Medieval West*, Oxford, 2002.

Charles Thomas & David Howlett, 'Vita Sancti Paterni: the Life of Saint Padarn and the Original "Miniu"', *Trivium*, Vol. 33, 2003.

A W Wade-Evans, *Vitae Sanctorum Britanniae et Genealogiae*, Cardiff, 1944.

A W Wade-Evans, *St. David, Archbishop, Patron of Wales*, from *The Cymmrodor* XX, 1913; republished in Stow-on-the-Wold, 1914.

A W Wade-Evans, *The Life of St David*, London, 1923.

Glanmor Williams, *Religion, Language and Nationality in Wales*, Cardiff, 1979.

J W Willis-Bund, *The Black Book of St David's*, London, 1902.

Edward Yardley, *Menevia Sacra* (ed. Francis Green), London, 1927.

Index

Saint David, his feast day and his biographer Rhygyfarch are not included, since they appear so often in the text. The chapter headings are a useful guide in this respect, as well as to such subjects as the Reformation and worship, poetry and pilgrimage.

Praise for
Ar Drywydd Dewi Sant

'Difyr, darllenadwy a diddorol'
(Entertaining, readable and interesting)

The Reverend Jeffrey Gainer

'Cefais flas anarferol ar y cyfan,
sy'n tystio i ddygnwch y chwilotwr hwn'

(I greatly enjoyed the whole book,
it's testimony to dedicated research)

Dr Bruce Griffiths

Also by the author:

A BRIEF
HISTORY
OF WALES

Gerald Morgan

y Lolfa

£4.95

Looking
for **Wales**

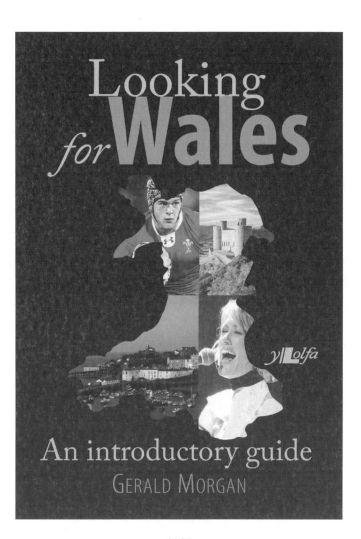

y Lolfa

An introductory guide
GERALD MORGAN

£4.95

In Pursuit of Saint David is just one of a whole
range of publications from Y Lolfa. For a full
list of books currently in print, send now
for your free copy of our new full-colour
catalogue. Or simply surf into our website

www.ylolfa.com

for secure on-line ordering.

TALYBONT CEREDIGION CYMRU SY24 5HE
e-mail ylolfa@ylolfa.com
website www.ylolfa.com
phone (01970) 832 304
fax 832 782